MU01057244

BROWN
WOMEN
HAVE
EVERYTHING

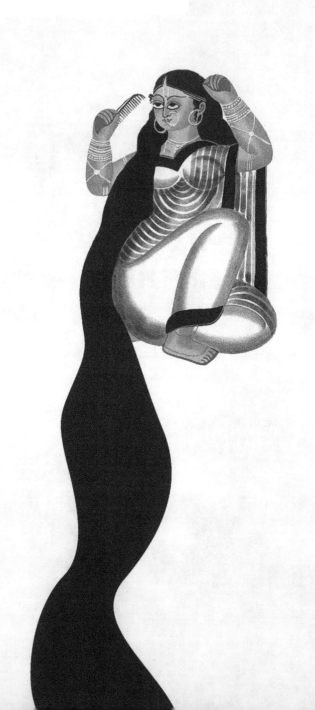

BROWN
WOMEN HAVE
EVERYTHING

ESSAYS ON
(DIS)COMFORT
AND DELIGHT

SAYANTANI DASGUPTA

THE UNIVERSITY OF NORTH CAROLINA PRESS
CHAPEL HILL

This book was published with
the assistance of the Greensboro Women's Fund
of the University of North Carolina Press.

Founding contributors: Linda Arnold Carlisle, Sally Schindel Cone,
Anne Faircloth, Bonnie McElveen Hunter, Linda Bullard Jennings,
Janice J. Kerley (in honor of Margaret Supplee Smith),
Nancy Rouzer May, and Betty Hughes Nichols.

© 2024 Sayantani Dasgupta
All rights reserved
Manufactured in the United States of America

Designed and set by Lindsay Starr in Alegreya

Cover art: Anwar Chitrakar, *Kalighat Patachitra 17*. Vegetable and
mineral colors on paper. Courtesy fineartamerica.com.

Complete Library of Congress Cataloging-in-Publication Data
is available at https://lccn.loc.gov/2024033090.

ISBN 9781469681764 (cloth: alk. paper)
ISBN 9781469681771 (pbk.: alk. paper)
ISBN 9781469681788 (epub)
ISBN 9781469681795 (pdf)

To my mother and grandmothers—
Swapna, Chhaya, and Minati Dasgupta.
Thank you for being my first friends,
teachers, and storytellers.

And for Kim Barnes—teacher, mentor, friend.
Thanks for teaching me how mining my memories
yields story after story.

CONTENTS

AUTHOR'S NOTE

IN HER ALMOST-FOUR YEARS thus far in our family, my sister-in-law Ashmita has heard so many stories about *my* stories that these days, anytime she hears yet another anecdote involving me, she asks a single, devastating question: "Didi, did this actually happen or is this another of your creations?"

To her, and others like her, I say, "Yes, all the stories in this book are true." However, for the sake of certain relationships, and because I am not a monster, I have changed names and identifying situations.

Other standard disclaimers of creative nonfiction follow: my recollection of events may or may not match those of others. They are, of course, welcome to tell their versions in the books they write, the tweets they tweet, and the missives they send to the universe.

January 2024

BROWN
WOMEN
HAVE
EVERYTHING

BECOMING THIS BROWN WOMAN, OR, THREE GLORIOUS ACCIDENTS

IT'S THE SUMMER OF 1976. Indira Gandhi is the prime minister of India, a company called Apple Computer is founded in California, and my maternal grandfather—though, as I am not yet born, he doesn't yet get to claim the title—posts an ad in the matrimonial column of *Ananda Bazaar Patrika*, the most-read newspaper in Kolkata (formerly Calcutta). Because its circulation is in the millions, he feels confident he will find a suitable match for his college-graduate daughter. An engineer, perhaps? Or maybe a doctor? All he and his wife want for her is a good boy from a good family. Well educated, of course.

As expected, his ad draws many letters in response. And why not? His daughter is nice to look at. She is well educated. They are a good, decent family. In other words, a perfect catch. One such letter is from the man who will become my paternal grandfather.

Dear Sir, the letter reads in Bengali, in his tidy and meticulous handwriting. *I am writing in response to your advertisement dated . . . I believe my son may be an excellent match for your daughter . . .*

IT'S THE WINTER OF 2021, and I am in Delhi, visiting my parents, when my mother pulls out these letters from the stainless-steel almirah she keeps in her bedroom. I am sprawled on her bed, on holiday from the rigors of my daily life in North Carolina, where I am a university professor. I have spent countless hours on this bed, ever since I was a kid, sprawled exactly like this, chatting with Ma, while watching her arrange and rearrange the contents of her almirah. The almirah is a treasure chest. A museum. It holds saris, sweaters, baby blankets, and jewelry, and even family photographs that Ma has deemed too old and frail to be tucked inside photo albums (remember those?).

When she hands the letters to me, I sit up to read them. I have to marvel at the penmanship of both of my grandfathers. Besides exquisite handwriting, they also shared a love for language, and, in fact, the same birthday, though not the same year: February 3.

The pages are a little worn and frayed, but the words are still bright and luminous. I am rereading the first-ever letter my paternal grandfather wrote to my maternal grandfather when the date catches my eye. "Look, look," I point excitedly.

"What?" Ma asks.

I jab at the date. It's my birthday, albeit three whole years *before* my actual birth.

My mother laughs, amused by this coincidence. I, on the other hand, want to believe cosmic powerhouses are at play here. The universe conspired to ensure that the very day one of my grandfathers reached out to the other, I arrived, three years later, on what I have been told was an exceptionally dark and stormy monsoon night in Kolkata. I want to believe that my grandfather knew even as he was writing the letter that his life was about to change, that his letter was going to be received favorably, and that a few months and meetings later, his son was going to get married.

You see, I am besotted with my birthday, and not in the polite, grown-up woman way one is expected to by the time they have crossed a certain age. No, I love my birthday like a five-year-old loves her birthday. I love it fiercely and ferociously. I want a massive song and dance about it. I want your letters and cards, I want a citrusy cake. I want all the dark chocolates, and tubes of nice hand creams. I will die for you if you gift me art supplies, especially the kind I feel guilty about buying for myself. So to me, the matter of the date is no mere coincidence. At the very least, it's my life's first most glorious accident.

THE SECOND SUCH ACCIDENT is the family into which I am born, the family I still get to call mine. I had a happy childhood, filled with books, readers, and storytellers, with people who valued education above all else. We lived simply. As was the norm in most middle-class families in India in the 1980s and 1990s, we rarely ate out. Restaurants hadn't taken over cities as they have now, like mushrooms sprouting after one good rain. Going out to watch a movie in a theater was a rare treat. My parents bought me new clothes only once or twice every year, usually before the annual five-day Durga Puja celebrations. I can't think of a single time in my life when I was growing up that I had more than a handful of outfits or, say, three or four pairs of shoes. Out-of-town trips were infrequent, and we almost always went to Kolkata to visit my grandparents during summer vacations.

But no one ever said no to me when it came to buying me yet another book.

I spoke Bengali at home, and Hindi and English at school and in the neighborhood. Because I was a voracious reader, I read in all three languages, and they cracked open the world, both near and far. It was astonishing to read an abridged version of *Twenty Thousand Leagues under the Sea* as a nine-year-old and learn that everything from the submarine *Nautilus* to its fetching leader Captain Nemo to the epic battles involving giant squids was the product of a single person's imagination. His name was Jules Verne, and his book was one of the first books of my life that made me intensely curious about what lay outside the realm of things and people I knew and could see. Who lived in places far away from mine? What did they do for fun? What did they eat if not the rice and fish curry that was the staple at my home?

For years, I read a book a day. I'd head home from school, change, eat lunch with Ma and my brother, and go for my afternoon nap.

Except I never napped. I read.

If one day I was tagging along with Hercule Poirot as he solved a murder along the Nile, the next day I was entwined in the vines of the monster plant in Satyajit Ray's *The Hungry Septopus* or helping the various gods of Hindu mythology fight off demons and save the rest of us.

Years later, when I left India for graduate studies in creative writing in the United States, a classmate—let's call him White Dude A— told another classmate—White Dude B—not to pay attention to any comments or critiques I made in the classroom, because according to him I was not well read enough to offer anything valuable. I heard about this conversation from White Dude C, who was friends with both of them. Although I can't know for sure, I imagine White Dude A arrived at this assessment based on something I had said in class just the week before, when my thirteen classmates and our professor were discussing that specific subgenre of American fiction known as Southern Gothic. I had sheepishly raised my hand, admitted to not knowing what it was, and said something along the lines of, "You will all have to forgive me. I am only two weeks old in America, so I don't yet know the writers who make up the American canon. Given India's colonial past, I am a bit more familiar with British authors. And with some of the writing in Bengali and Hindi."

In hindsight, I think White Dudes A and B *should* have paid attention to what I had to say in the classroom. For one, it would have been the professional thing to do. Also, decent and kind. More importantly, especially from the perspective of writers and readers everywhere, I represented a worldview they might not have come across on their own. I was the only non-American student in my creative writing program and one of three students of color.

Could the same thing happen today? Of course. Anything is possible in a private conversation, though I want to believe we are more enlightened now. Back then, in 2006, the world *was* different. Twitter had just been launched. Tom Cruise and Katie Holmes were contemplating a loving future together. The most popular television show in the US was *Desperate Housewives*. While new words such as "crowdfunding" and "crowdsourcing" had just entered our lexicon, we had not invented hashtags. So we didn't know how to be in the world and behave with each other. Those two classmates were also friends with others in the program who looked and behaved exactly like them. Together, they made workshops difficult for anyone they considered an outsider. Perhaps if they had paid attention to what I had to say, who knows, they too might have published a book or two by now.

THE THIRD AND FINAL glorious accident of my life is my parents' move to New Delhi from Kolkata in 1985, when my father landed a new job. I was five years old. To an outsider, I imagine New Delhi and Kolkata represent two cities in India that are indistinguishable from each other. But back then, especially in pre-internet days, they were like two different countries.

Even at five, I understood how unmoored my parents felt in this new city, with this new life. Suddenly the main language of communication was no longer Bengali; it was Hindi. It was a challenge to find the kind of fresh fruits and vegetables they had taken for granted in Kolkata. They were now exclusively in charge of their own lives and mine. We had moved from our multigenerational home in Kolkata, where my grandparents had presided over everything, to this new world, where they now had to figure out how to be parents and their own persons.

I am sure I learned a lot, even if only subconsciously, from my parents' discomfort. I learned that there is honor and dignity in pursuing your dreams, in moving out of places and worlds that are comfortable and familiar, in making mistakes, and perhaps even in being homesick.

It seems impossible to imagine this now, as I dictate notes for this essay to my phone, but back in 1985, every home did not have a phone. Our home in Delhi certainly didn't. Even if we had had one, calling my grandparents in Kolkata at will would have been impossible. For one, it was prohibitively expensive. For another, calls dropped all the time. Everyone in India relied on letters—pale yellow postcards that cost fifteen paises, blue inlands worth fifty paises, or sealed envelopes that cost a full rupee's worth of stamp. You wrote the letter, dropped the letter in the letter box, and waited until the other person received it, processed its contents in their minds, and wrote back. Then you read that letter and replied. And so on and so forth. Somewhere in the middle of all this, if you ran out of stamps or postcards, you physically went to the post office to buy some, and that was its own adventure.

At my home, Saturdays were the designated day for my father to race through the list of chores and errands that he couldn't tend to during the workweek. Sundays were no good. Everything was closed on Sundays. On Saturdays, I would accompany Baba as he paid off sundry bills and picked up, say, medicines, a new hammer to replace the old one, the mutton Ma had said we would eat for Sunday's lunch, and the ten-kilo bag of rice that would have been impossible for her to haul back home on her own.

The post office was always our last stop. I imagine it was Baba's least favorite place to go. Understandably so. I can't remember a single time when the men and women on the other side of the desk made the experience quick or easy or polite. I imagine that at least in their initial years in Delhi, such experiences exacerbated the overall discomfort my parents felt with the city.

In my own way, I experienced similar discomfort when I moved to the US in 2006. So desperate had I been to study creative writing that I accepted the spot I was offered at a university in Idaho without any hesitation. It came with no funding. I had no money for a laptop, and while I had had a cell phone back home, affording one here was out of the question.

The local post office, though, was a treat. The men and women always looked you in the eye, greeted you with a smile, and cheerfully asked what they could do for you.

IN VERY SIMPLISTIC TERMS, it feels like everything that has happened in my life has been the result of these three glorious accidents. From the institutions where I studied in India and in the US; to the man I met and married in Idaho in a small ceremony where we were surrounded by thirty of our closest friends and family; to the jobs I have held; to all the small, random moments like that time I picked blackberries in a parking lot in Port Townsend, Washington, where each fruit tasted as ripe and fulfilling as a happy tear; to the week I spent in Bogota, Colombia, awed by the range of its graffiti and street art; to that night I got lost on my way back to my hotel in Florence, Italy, and got catcalled by Bangladeshi vendors, and in that instant my body and mind rerouted me to New Delhi, to the ordeal of negotiating its streets as a teenager, unsure if being a girl meant that I belonged to myself, or to the entire world and its relentless scrutiny and observation.

That girl has long since been replaced by a woman. But that scrutiny is still here though it has taken on different forms. Most recently I faced it inside a classroom, where I had been invited to deliver a guest lecture. About seventy or eighty students were in attendance. I read an excerpt from my first book and answered a slew of questions.

Just as we were about to wrap up, a blond girl raised her hand. Dressed in shorts and a T-shirt, she looked like many others in the audience. "I don't have a question," she said, slowly, doubt clouding her face and voice. "It's more of a comment, really. You have a lot of confidence."

It was an odd declaration. A strange sentence. Most certainly not a compliment. I wonder if what she meant to say was, How are you this confident when you are short, overweight, and so different from what I think a college professor should look like?

Her comment didn't make me angry. It reminded me of a faculty-staff event I attended soon after accepting my current job, where two white ladies introduced themselves, shook hands with me, looked me up and down, and, by way of making conversation, said, "Of course you got the job. Brown women have everything these days. They get all the jobs." I had looked around the room, at the 300 or so people in attendance, of whom only a handful were Black or brown, and told them that they were wrong.

I was also reminded of questions I used to have as a kid, when I would devour travel shows on the National Geographic and Discovery channels. More than the wondrous places themselves, I was in love with the hosts. They were always young, energetic, and confident, with perfect smiles and teeth. They were magical creatures who got to travel to other countries, sample cuisines, immerse themselves in cultures different from their own, and tell the rest of us how to feel about these places and people. At that time, I knew nothing of terms such as "accessibility" or "privilege." All I wondered was, how did all the explorers know they had to be white? Couldn't the rest of us be this courageous or curious about the world?

These days, while I continue to reflect on questions about TV shows and who gets to travel where and tell us what, I also know that courage and curiosity are fluid concepts. No one person or people or profession can claim monopoly over them. It's not really about wild adventures in foreign lands. Instead, it's about going against the grain, trying things one hasn't tried before.

This may take the form of wild imaginings, such as a book about an eccentric sea captain and a submarine that runs entirely on electricity. How curious that nearly 120 years after its publication, a nine-year-old received this book on her birthday and, sitting on her bed in landlocked New Delhi, she too imagined epic battles with giant squids, and the thrill of creating and containing entire worlds and people inside the vessel of her head.

At other times, curiosity and courage may take the form of rebuilding your life in a new city. Or learning a new language. Or stepping inside a classroom or a faculty-staff event where only a few people look like you.

Or perhaps it is 1976 and a trip to the nearest post office. It's a different experience than what you typically undergo. The clerk is polite and smiles when you ask to purchase a single stamp. You write many letters in any given week, so it's not a daunting task per se. But this letter is different. You have written it with greater care than usual. You are hoping it will impress a stranger enough that he will marry off his daughter to your son. At least you have chosen the best, most cosmically approved day of the year, because your granddaughter will be born on this day—granted, three years into the future. Sure, some people, including a few in your own family, will dismiss this as mere coincidence, but you, in your heart of hearts, must know what you are setting in motion.

I imagine Jules Verne would approve. For on this *same* day in 1892, he received the Légion d'honneur, the highest order of merit in France. It was awarded to Verne for his many contributions to arts and letters, and, though neither officially mentioned nor acknowledged, for igniting imaginations.

MANE STORY

ONCE UPON A TIME, long before I came to the United States, I was in love with my hair. It was thick, wavy, and lush. I had inherited good hair genes from both my parents, and they in turn from theirs. "It's all the fish in our collective DNA," my mother would say. I believed her because it was true. Generations of men and women in my family had lived along the rivers and ponds whose waters fed the Bay of Bengal, so presumably my ancestors did eat fish every day, perhaps for nearly every meal. As a kid, whenever this subject came up in conversation, I conjured up sumptuous, pastoral images in my head: of men stepping out with their fishing poles and nets and returning home with ample catches, and the women taking those same fish and frying, sautéing, currying them up so everyone could savor them with mountains of white rice, shiny-with-sting green chilies, slowly melting dollops of homemade ghee, and limes plucked straight from the garden for slicing into delicate half-moons.

So what if I myself was growing up in landlocked New Delhi, far away from Bengal and its fish-rich waters? My ancestors' blessings still reached me. Thanks to them, I had hair that framed my face and never needed combing. Of course, it helped that, like them, I ate fish every day. No, not for breakfast. But definitely for lunch and dinner, Monday through Friday, because on weekends we ate chicken or mutton. It didn't matter that we didn't live near water. All we had to do was cross the street and go to the nearest market. Fish, ghee, limes that could be sliced into half-moons—everything was within easy reach.

I hit my best hair years when I was a teenager. I could wash it with any soap or shampoo—not that there were many choices in India in the mid-1990s, nor did we have conditioners or serums or whatever else became available in the next few years.

But you know what? My hair didn't care. It was always ready to bounce, and I took it for granted along with the hundreds of compliments I received for it over the years. Back then, I didn't like most things that made me *me*. I didn't like my size or my nose. I didn't like that my fingers weren't long enough, or that my legs were so squat. I didn't like the length of my neck or that my feet were so broad.

My hair, though? My hair had my heart.

Until, that is, I arrived in the US.

THE YEAR WAS 2006. I was in my mid-twenties. A graduate student of creative writing at the University of Idaho, I was broke, in the manner of most students I knew and respected. My two on-campus jobs barely covered my rent, and in my new hometown of Moscow, Idaho, I had to let go of several daily fixtures of my life. I now ate fish rarely, and when I did, I purchased it from the frozen section of the nearest gigantic grocery store, whose every aisle felt way too cold and smelled of, well, nothing. Not a single item emitted any aroma, yet every shelf bore food. The local co-op showed far more life and animation, and in fact sold fresh fish every Friday, but anything from there was out of my budget.

Same with haircuts. Especially once I learned that paying for the trim alone would not be enough. I would now have to top it with a tip.

Not just once or twice if the service was exceptional, but every single time. So I let my hair be, until the day finally arrived when I realized I had saved enough. Triumphant and a little nervous—because going to a salon feels exactly like going to the doctor wherein a hundred problems you didn't know you had are yanked out of the deepest recesses of your body—I found myself a hairdresser.

Let's say her name was Maggie.

Maggie was in her early forties. She was a white lady, with blond hair that had vivid red streaks. She wore black jeans with a matching T-shirt. She had a generous smile, and she sat me down in a comfortable chair in front of a large mirror. So far, so good. This was going exactly like all salon visits back home. Like the women and men who had cut my hair before, Maggie carried a pair of shears in one hand and a comb in the other.

With her left hand, she began assessing the task in front of her. She may have been humming a tune. I may have closed my eyes, allowing myself to relax in the delight that is someone running their fingers through your hair.

I wasn't prepared for what came next.

"*Hon*-ney," Maggie drawled. "You have some seriously coarse hair."

I don't remember what I said in reply. Or if I said anything at all. I remember being taken aback by her use of the word "coarse." What did that mean? Can anyone's *hair* really be coarse? Could *my* hair be coarse? Of course, I was familiar with the word itself. I had heard it before. No doubt, I had used it too. If I needed to describe, say, freshly ground peppercorns. Or black pumice stones with which you scrubbed off dead skin from your heels. Sandpaper. Burlap sacks that transported coffee. Fish scales. But hair? How could hair be coarse?

I am sure I said something self-deprecating, so that the moment didn't become awkward, so that Maggie didn't feel bad about her assessment. But this I remember: the following month, with money I could barely afford, I went to Ross Dress for Less and bought myself a hair straightener.

I spoke to a friend shortly after my purchase. I said, "You know what? I really should get into the habit of ironing my hair every morning, so it is straight and polished the whole day instead of the mess it becomes."

My friend, a white woman my age with curly blond hair, raised her eyebrows. "You don't think curly hair can look polished?"

I rushed to explain. "No, no. Of course not. Your kind of curly hair can definitely look polished. Yours is beautiful and manageable. Mine needs help. Mine is coarse."

LATELY, PERHAPS because of the pandemic that's led me (and others) to spend extraordinary amounts of time at home and inside one's head, or perhaps because I am now in my forties and have strands of gray, or perhaps because I am forever listing things to write about, I have been thinking a lot about hair. About how that phase with the straightener lasted for only a few months until I got bored with the routine. It now sits inside a blue box in my bathroom, where it is neighbors with extra toothbrushes and tubes of toothpaste, soaps of all sizes, and mini-moisturizers pilfered from good hotels by my husband. Now that I no longer live in dry Idaho but in coastal North Carolina, where humidity is a constant, I probably need that straightener more than I have ever needed it before. Here my hair is truly an unruly beast, refusing to be tamed or subject to reason, unless I woo it first with industrial quantities of coconut and grapeseed oil.

I have also been thinking about the hair of the women in my family.

For example, Ma, my mother, whose hair is still beautiful. I have heard countless stories of her thick, waist-length hair eliciting envy among her friends and cousins when they were all growing up. From the photographs I have seen of my parents' wedding, I know Ma wore it in a bun that day, and it sat at the back of her neck, decked with flowers.

Or Thamma, my paternal grandmother, who combed and coconut-oiled her hair every evening after she rose from her afternoon nap. She would change into a fresh sari; wash and moisturize her face with Oil of Olay that her younger sister regularly shipped to her from Newcastle, England; and then lightly dab her face, neck, and shoulders with powder, all in time for my grandfather's return from work. She did this every day without fail, not just for him—the love of her life—but also for herself and for the steady stream of visitors that was a given in my grandparents' home no matter the time of the year.

I have also been thinking of my other grandmother. Dida, my mother's mother. Gone now for over twenty years. But in the way your loved ones never really go but sort of continue to live in the air around you, I often hear her voice. She calls out the nickname that was hers to use for me, and I recognize that laugh that used to roll off her in waves.

In my mind's eye, Dida appears exactly as I have always known her. Her face is round and smooth, unlined by wrinkles, and her shoulder-length hair is tied in a braid. I remember how some nights, when we were visiting her home in Kolkata or she was visiting us in New Delhi, Dida would have me comb her hair right before she went to sleep. Or on lazy afternoons while watching TV she'd have me pluck the curly white strands closest to her face.

From the way she reminisced about how her hair used to be when she was young, I understand now that it must have been her crowning glory. Back then, I don't know if I really listened, if I paid her the attention I should have, or if, in the manner of teenagers everywhere, I was impatient to get on with whatever distraction—friend, book, or boy—had claimed my attention for the day.

I never met Dida's husband, my maternal grandfather. He passed away two years before my birth. But I got to know his absence because Dida followed practices expected of high-caste Hindu widows. She never wore any makeup. She wore slight jewelry—tiny gold studs in her ears, thin gold bangles on her wrists. Her go-to saris were in light colors, cotton for everyday wear, silk for fancy occasions. Never any bright fabrics or elaborate designs.

Still, because this was the 1980s and '90s, and because I come from a progressive family, Dida could choose to follow or discard any of the rules she wanted. But say we were to go back just two generations. Say, instead of being born in 1929, Dida had been born in 1889. What kind of rules and restrictions would have been imposed on her—a widow—then?

Rule 1: Wear plain, unspun, cotton saris. All day. Every day. No color. Just white, the color of mourning in Hinduism.

Rule 2: Eat a diet made up of boiled vegetables and unpolished rice. No meat. No fish. No fried foods. No sweets. Meat was a rare treat for most people in Bengal back then, so I imagine its absence wouldn't have made much of a difference. But fish? The mainstay of Bengali cuisine? How was one supposed to survive without it?

Rule 3: Never attend weddings or other social events, because a widow's presence was "unlucky." Of course, the same gathering could potentially host hundreds of widowers without anyone raising an eyebrow.

Rule 4: Never wear any jewelry or makeup.

Rule 5: Shave head regularly. Because if a woman's husband is dead, so should her desire to live and look presentable, and what better way of ensuring that than to take off all her hair?

THE ELEVENTH-CENTURY Persian fairy tale "Zal and Rudabeh" has much to do with hair. Rudabeh, the Princess of Kabul, falls in love with the legendary warrior Zal. Her friends tease her because Zal, though young, has hair that's turned white. When Zal travels to meet Rudabeh, she is high up in her tower and offers to let down her hair so he may climb up. He refuses, so as not to hurt her, and suggests she let down a rope instead.

Of course, you might be more familiar with the German iteration of the story, "Rapunzel," first published in 1812. Or with *Tangled*, the American computer-animated adventure film from 2010. It's replete with great songs, a compassionate yet plucky heroine, a magnificent horse that's more like a dog, and a charming rogue of a hero.

In *Tangled*, when Rapunzel sings, her hair glows, and when it glows, it can heal wounds, erase signs of aging, shine underwater, and of course, support the weight of adult men and women with no visible trauma or injury to her scalp. It is her hair that leads the witch to kidnap Rapunzel when she is still a baby, and it is the loss of this same hair as an adult that finally sets her free and reunites her with her family.

I have to wonder about this journey that Rudabeh or Rapunzel made, from Persia to Germany to California. What if, instead of traveling to the West, she had traveled to the East? Let's keep the year constant. Let's say it's still 1889 but the destination is Kolkata.

Would the absence of a husband have made her much sought after? Or would her long, lustrous hair have gotten her branded as a "witch," thereby inviting the wrath of upper-caste, upper-class Brahmin men, along with the English officers in charge of Kolkata at that time? How dare she grow her hair this long? How dare she look different from the mothers and daughters and wives they had at home, women who were soft and smooth, who did delicate things like embroider? How dare she be different from the norm? How dare she be coarse?

I am also thinking of Joan of Arc. Before she was burned at the stake, her executioners shaved her head. Historians say her hair had already been short to begin with because she didn't want it to interfere with her military career or cause a distraction among fellow soldiers. But clearly that wasn't enough. Before she was killed, her executioners wanted to strip her of even the tiniest semblance of individuality.

But let's say Rapunzel didn't go to Kolkata. That in 1889 she went to New York instead. Would she have fared any better? Debatable.

A girl like her, meaning, a girl on her own, might have been taken into the "protective custody" of an institution such as the House of Mercy at Inwood, a reform school for "bad characters." Run by Episcopalian nuns, it housed girls and young women who were rebellious or runaways or made their living as sex workers or club dancers. The nuns' favorite forms of punishments for unruly wards included reducing the size of their rations. That, and cutting off their hair.

EVEN NOW, more than a hundred years later, a woman with a shaved head is a mystery. Is she unwell? Or rebellious? Why can't she be "normal" like everyone else? Why is she asking to be turned into a joke or a meme or some such personal attack?

Remember when Britney Spears shaved her head in 2007? Perhaps it was because she did it in full view of everyone on national television that she was compared to "a three-year-old throwing a tantrum." Some of her critics accused her of trying to detract attention from her addictions. Others joked and said her career was over. I remember I was in New York that day, at John F. Kennedy International Airport, on my way back from India at the end of my monthlong winter break. I was waiting impatiently for my next, much-delayed connecting flight to take me back to Idaho. The trip to India had been splendid. I had stayed mostly at home and soaked up time with my immediate family. I had hung out with close friends. I had eaten my favorite foods. I had even managed a trip or two to my favorite salon, where, after an enthusiastic check-in, they had washed and cut my hair. No one, not a single person, had called it coarse: there, my hair's texture is the norm and not the anomaly.

At JFK, every moment that I was not checking the status of my flight, my eyes automatically landed on the gigantic TV screens. Britney was everywhere. Scorned Britney. Insulted Britney. Ridiculed Britney. All because she had simply picked up a razor and shaved her head.

IN HIS BOOK *Shorn Women: Gender and Punishment in Liberation France*, the historian Fabrice Virgili examines the nature of collaboration between German soldiers and French women during World War II. He writes that nearly 20,000 women were accused of cohabiting with these soldiers, and after the war, humiliating punishments were meted out to them in public. Stripped to their underwear, they were paraded through the streets. Their faces and bodies were marked with swastikas and their heads shaved.

They were called *les femme tondues*, "the shorn women."

Virgili writes that there was little evidence to prove that these women had in fact willingly slept with German soldiers and that during the six years of war they hadn't been victims of rape or coercion. The public nature of these punishments was, in fact, a combination of a defense strategy and a reaction to the humiliation and suffering incurred by the French during the German Occupation. These women were easy targets, and their faces, bodies, and hair bore the brunt of it.

In my home in Wilmington, North Carolina, on days when I know I am not stepping out, I gather my hair and tie it in a loose ponytail or heap it in a lopsided bun on top of my head. Some days I think about that straightener and debate whether to keep or donate it. Who knows?—some other broke, coarse-haired person might find a use for it.

On days when I have to oil or comb or condition my hair, I end up thinking about the women whose hands have nurtured my hair. My mother. My favorite hairdressers. Both my grandmothers. And the mothers and grandmothers who came before them, women I never met in person but whose DNA swims with mine. Women who may have kept their hair irrespective of their marital status, and women who had to shave it off, who couldn't keep their curls and waves, their braids and buns, coarse or otherwise. Women who didn't get to choose the course of their lives or drop everything in their mid-twenties just so they could go abroad and study creative writing.

If only they could see me. How strange and impractical I must appear to them. How indulgent and wasteful they must think I am because I get to play with words and give in to my imagination.

But it is this very imagination that allows me to imagine them staging mini-rebellions. I see them sneaking into the kitchen when no one's around, no one's watching, and steal pickled mangos. Each sliver drips with mustard oil, and spices so rich and red they might just stain one's fingernails. But so what? Repeat, tomorrow. No, don't go for the mango pickle again. Aim for something bigger. Better. A more satisfying mouthful. Fried fish, perhaps. Caught in the waters just outside the house. Still juicy inside, and the outside armored in crisp batter, a marriage if you will, of sweet, desiccated coconut with a slather of turmeric and mustard seeds, fresh yet coarsely ground.

RINSE, REPEAT

SEPTEMBER 2018.

It's the email from my apartment-leasing company that alerts me to the severity of the situation. For days now, I have been watching the slow build of Hurricane Florence, a dense white clot over the Atlantic Ocean, a menacing eye, much like the eye of Sauron. Satellite images show landfall will be in four days, in Wilmington, North Carolina, my home for the past month, a touristy beach city of about 100,000 residents. Thus far, several longtime residents have assured me this isn't that out of the norm during our annual "hurricane season." That we have something called hurricane season, in effect from June 1 to November 30, is in and of itself deeply alarming.

But I am here now. What's the point in scaring myself any more than necessary? I have heard it said over and over again that most hurricanes are fairly "anticlimactic." Almost "boring." All they cause are a lot of rain, punctuated by power cuts.

However, the manager's email, with the subject line "Get Ready for Hurricane Florence" and divided into three sections, listing twenty-five points in all, is something else. It is a manifesto. A call and plan for action. I reread the instructions, and although many do not apply to me—I don't have to bring in my plants or patio furniture because I don't own any—the visual heft of them tightens something inside me.

A Facebook notification pops up. It's a message from James, one of my former students from Idaho, where I used to teach before, and who now lives in Greenville, North Carolina, two or so hours away from the coast. He is a middle school English teacher these days, and shortly after my arrival, he had driven down to eat lunch with me. Inside an Irish-themed restaurant, we had relived our memories of Idaho, and listening to him talk passionately about teaching and his students had easily been one of the best welcome-to-Wilmington experiences.

"Come to Greenville," James's message says. "We are sufficiently inland. This one looks big."

I turn off my laptop and step out into the balcony. For the thousandth time, I wish I wasn't dealing with this on my own. I wish my husband was here. He had been, for the first two weeks, helping me settle into my new life and apartment, the latter selected sight unseen, based purely on its location. A twelve-minute walk to my department on campus, a short drive to the ocean in one direction, and about the same in the opposite direction if, instead of the beach, you wanted to hang out in Wilmington's historic downtown.

But now he has returned to our home and his job in Idaho. He will join me in three months, by which time he'd have wrapped up things at work and packed the remainder of our belongings. That was the plan until Florence came calling. Now, I don't know.

I lean against the railing. Miraculously, there is a breeze, a respite from the usual humidity, a rare moment of being outside and not slathered in a film of sweat. My husband joked nearly every day that he was here, "Breathing in Wilmington is like being inside a whale's mouth. Sticky, smelly, unforgiving."

Neither of us is used to this level of humidity. We are products of drier cities. He is from Los Angeles, I am from New Delhi. We met, fell in love, and got married in Moscow, Idaho. It was hard to believe at times that we had built our lives in a place so astonishingly beautiful. Moscow was green and lush with wildflowers in spring, dry and arid in summer, cold and rainy in fall with leaves turning orange, red, and fire; and snowy and icy from November to March. Wilmington, North Carolina, is our first experience of the South. Wilmingtonians have warned us that it is humid here year-round, and that we will want the air conditioner on for at least six of those months.

I grab the railing with my hands and breathe in deeply. Beyond the line of trees and apartments, some fifteen minutes away, there is the Atlantic Ocean and, hovering over it, Hurricane Florence. But you wouldn't think that looking at the gently swaying, skinny branches of the pines, or today's clear blue sky, the kind of blue you long for on the best day of your life.

THE FIRST TIME I walked along Wrightsville Beach, I called my mother on WhatsApp. I wanted her help in choosing my new desk. I was split between two options that I had come across at a consignment store. Made of solid cherry in the 1950s, both desks had been refurbished. The first was painted gray and brown; the second, olive green. Ma helped me choose (the olive green), and we continued chatting for an hour, her from landlocked Delhi, and me with the Atlantic in my background.

During his time here, for three mornings in a row, my husband and I went to the beach to watch the sun rise. We stuffed our pockets with gifts—shells, sea glass, smooth stones, gnarled bits that looked like fossilized bones, and teeth of prehistoric, unknowable animals. All through our move, my husband had said that his first task upon seeing the Atlantic in person would be to heckle it. Having lived in Los Angeles most of his life, "his" ocean would always be the Pacific. No way would the Atlantic match its magnitude.

But at that first sight, its sheer enormity made him forget his previous resolve. "This is my favorite moment," he said quietly.

I couldn't bring myself to say anything. I just nodded. We had arrived in Wilmington, exhausted and broken from the packing, angry and impatient with the move and with each other. For the last several weeks, we had survived on Domino's pizzas, our lives dominated by bubble wrap, tape, rolls of brown paper, movers who didn't always answer their phones, and employers that didn't pay for moving expenses, not even for this cross-country move from Idaho to North Carolina.

But the ocean took it all away. It absorbed our exhaustion and put us in better moods. Each morning, no matter what state of mind we were in when we arrived at the beach, we left holding hands, ready for the day in our new home.

I'VE WANTED THIS ALL MY LIFE, this proximity to the ocean, ever since reading *Twenty Thousand Leagues under the Sea* at age nine and falling in love with Captain Nemo. Ever since imagining the same life for my family as the one in *Swiss Family Robinson* and praying that a similar adventure would buoy us to a remote island far, far away. Ever since dragging my then-boyfriend, now-husband to Point Arena Lighthouse, in Mendocino County, California, for a holiday, where we paid through our noses to stay for three nights at the former keeper's quarters. Every morning we drank our coffees by the edge of the sheer cliff, our words drowned by the roar of the Pacific, while harbor seals glistened and rock-bathed all the way below.

Earlier this year, when I was informed that I was a finalist for the job at Wilmington and that I would have to come down for an in-person, all-day interview, replete with presentations and meetings with deans, graduate students, and potential colleagues, I had hoped I would have time to visit Wrightsville, the nearest beach. Imagine my joy on discovering that the hotel where they put me up was on Wrightsville Beach and that my fourth-floor room faced the ocean. I didn't have to go anywhere to visit the Atlantic. It was right there—gray, limitless, and powerful.

I have been an atheist since I was fifteen, largely because of my refusal to believe in something I can't see. The Atlantic, however, does not present such a problem. On the morning of my interview, I prayed to the ocean. How could I not? It stretched from my line of sight all the way to infinity. I could sense its power from my safe distance away on solid ground. It made me feel small and insignificant, the way the Grand Canyon had a few years ago, or the Taj Mahal when I had last visited it as a teenager. And while I wouldn't recommend feeling small and insignificant, especially not before a career-making interview, because these emotions were brought on by the Atlantic, they sat just right.

BUT IT'S ONE THING to love lighthouses and books set in the sea, and quite another to face up to hurricanes. And Florence is supposed to be a big one. Experts have predicted it will be a Category 4 hurricane with the potential of turning into a 5. Hurricane Katrina was a 5. It killed nearly 2,000 people and kept New Orleans inundated for weeks.

What does Category 5 mean for Wilmington? Widespread flooding, sandwiched as it is by the Atlantic Ocean on one side and the less-than-cheerful-sounding Cape Fear River on the other. Massive power outages. Fierce winds uprooting hundreds of trees, toppling and ripping apart homes and other properties, not to mention the potential loss of lives.

And what does it mean for my two-bedroom, third-floor apartment? According to the simulation video shared by a local hurricane-watch group I have joined on Facebook, I will lose my roof to high winds; I could lose access to water, electricity, and the internet; any of the neighboring pine trees could crash onto my building or sail in through a window, unleashing rain and other debris onto my just-purchased furniture, pots and pans, and all the accoutrements that go into turning an apartment into a home.

This move, from Moscow, Idaho, to Wilmington, North Carolina, has spanned a distance of approximately 2,800 miles. It has devoured my savings. In the whirlpool that's been cross-country travel, the weeklong orientation program, and the slew of classes I'm teaching for the first time, I have forgotten to buy renter's insurance. If this apartment goes, it will take with it everything I own.

LET'S PAUSE HERE A MOMENT.

It's true I know nothing about hurricanes, but may I interest you in a class on how to write? That's the job that's brought me here. I am a professor of creative writing at the local, public university. I can teach you all you need to know about different kinds of essays—flash, memoir, narrative, segmented, collage. I can recommend books you should read to strengthen your authorial voice or tighten your narrative arc. I will share with you my strategies for writing strong dialogue, and I can talk to you for hours on why you must read a lot of fiction and poetry even if you are committed to writing only nonfiction every day of your life.

In my time here so far, as was bound to happen, I have settled into a semi-routine: on weekends, I shop and cook, I watch movies, and I share a meal or two with my new colleagues. On weekdays, once I am done teaching my undergrads, I walk the five or so minutes from my office to the campus library. I am immediately at home here, anchored with one book or more at the coffee shop conveniently located inside. Here I grade, I meet with students, I read, research, and write, and chat with colleagues, not just from my department but also from others, like Mathematics, who write warm, welcoming emails to me after reading my profile in the "New Hires" newsletter blasted to all faculty, staff, and students.

I am constantly homesick for Idaho, for my apartment on Main Street, and the cafés where I wrote my first book and met up with friends, for the warm and cozy bookstores where the owners and staff knew my name, the incredible restaurants steps away from my door, and those friendly strangers who made up life in Moscow.

Here, in Wilmington, I am years away from re-creating the robust community of friends my husband and I had gotten used to. Here most of my evenings are mine alone. Once I am done on campus, I walk home, while my husband stays on the phone with me. I try not to tell him about my loneliness, so I tell him about my students instead, about how energized I feel by their questions, and by the depth of their commitment to becoming better writers and readers.

But then there are other days, usually after I teach my three-hour-long, graduate-level workshop, when I return home feeling

24

overwhelmed, drained, and completely out of my depth. I have not taught at this level before, and given that several of my students are not that much younger, I am convinced they know as much as me about writing. So I imagine their derision. I wonder if they have nicknames for me the way I used to for my professors when I was in college. I worry they will speak to the chair of the department and tell him I am not needed here.

On those evenings, I sit in front of the TV for hours, watching-not-watching reruns of *The Office*, scrolling, scrolling, scrolling on my phone, leaping from one social media app to another, here a birthday wish, there a cat video, unwilling, unable, to even get up and wash my face, forget about fixing dinner, or getting to sleep on time so as to be ready for my early morning class the next day, all the while playing in my mind everything I should have said and done but didn't, the ways I should have exerted my authority and scholarship but didn't, filling up my mind with the kind of self-loathing I have rarely experienced before.

When I share my doubts with a senior colleague, she smiles. She assures me I am doing okay. But my doubts remain. If anything, they burrow deeper. They ask nonstop, "Do you really think this is fine? Is this all one can expect from you?"

LIKE EVERY OTHER PLACE ON EARTH, Wilmington is complicated. It's the site of the only coup d'état in US history. On November 10, 1898, two days after a democratically elected government came to power, it was overthrown and replaced by white supremacists; at least sixty people were killed, and the building that housed the *Daily Record*, a Black-owned and -run newspaper, was torched. Today the site of what was once North Carolina's only African American newspaper is an ordinary parking lot.

Downtown Wilmington, where many events of the Massacre of 1898 unfolded, still carried bronze statues commemorating Confederate soldiers and politicians such as George Davis, whose speech in 1861 recommended that North Carolina secede from the country to preserve its right to allow slavery. (These statues were removed in 2020.)

Not that I am surprised by this. I know how history functions. I understand the role of erasure and remembrance, as a student of both history and literature, and because I am from Delhi, one of the oldest cities in the world, built, extended, and rebuilt on the ruins of former dynasties by the whims of whoever is in power. I also know that attitudes and prejudices don't die just because they should. Often, they linger, and raise their heads unexpectedly.

Perhaps that explains why in my one month here, I have heard so many horror stories from my Black students. "I don't go downtown if my date is white," one of them said. "They look at you weird. You could be inside one of those nice restaurants, you know, with twinkling lights and all, or you could walk down the riverfront, grand and old and historic, and they will still look at you funny."

Or why a senior colleague, a woman of color from another department, said, "My husband and I avoid downtown if we can. We get stares every, single time. You be careful too."

Physical ramifications of the hurricane aside, I, a brown woman, do not want to be by myself if Florence brings Wilmington to its knees. In a stretched-thin-for-resources, predominantly white city, I worry who will survive and who will be sacrificed. When Hurricane Katrina lashed Florida, Mississippi, and Louisiana in 2005, I was still in India. I remember seeing the many images of looting and rioting in the news. I remember my then-boyfriend's smirks: "Americans should stop calling themselves a first-world nation. It's easy to imagine such crimes in developing countries like India, especially after a natural disaster. Look at them now. They are just as uncivilized as the rest of us."

Though I have now lived in the US for nearly two decades, there are times in any given day when I still feel out of place, when I wonder if I am being too familiar or inappropriate, if I am crossing a line of American etiquette or social norm that I, as a foreign woman, should not. *Did I smile enough? Did I show up on time? Did I say "sorry," "please," and "thank you" the right number of times?*

In the back-and-forth of emails, texts, and messages that Florence unleashes upon us, a colleague I reach out to never replies, but four others check in on me on their own. Two even offer me places to stay.

I am touched. This is a stressful time for everyone, no matter how long they have lived in this city or how many hurricanes they have faced. That anyone has paused in between whatever steps they need to take to safeguard their homes and families just to make sure I am doing okay is very kind.

AS NERVOUS AS I AM, the uniqueness of my situation isn't lost on me. I, the granddaughter of refugees, am keenly aware that evacuation is its own privilege. Back in 1947, after the partition of India upon gaining independence, my grandparents from both sides were forced out of homes they had lived in for generations. They fled to Kolkata, from what was then East Pakistan, and rebuilt their lives from scratch. But along the way they lost friends and family, a language or two, and items that had made them who they were in the first place. *We gave away rooms full of books. Hardbound with gold lettering on the spine.* Their stories of surviving on rice water, of standing in unending lines in hopes of food and shelter, of days spent simply waiting, are as much my inheritance as my language or surname are. And still, all through my time with them, my grandparents insisted they were "the lucky ones." They didn't talk much about those on whom mobs descended, who didn't or couldn't evacuate.

I WEIGH MY OPTIONS through every lens I own—the good, the bad, the absolutely nonsensical.

I am reluctant to rent a hotel room in Raleigh or Durham, my nearest safe cities. I don't know how long Wilmington will remain unapproachable. I don't know how long I will be able to afford a hotel if recovery extends from a matter of days to weeks.

What would Captain Nemo say? He, my first literary crush; tall, erudite, and bearded; the son of an Indian prince; and the hero of *Twenty Thousand Leagues under the Sea.* What kind of person insists she is excited by all the maritime history surrounding Wilmington, including the fact that were he still alive, the notorious pirate Blackbeard would practically be her neighbor—there is apparently even a museum dedicated to him two hours from here—but runs away at the first sign of trouble?

When I call my husband, he is in no mood for discussion. "I am buying you a ticket," he says. We look at prices, and I recoil as if I have been struck. Given the demand and urgency of the situation, tickets are few, and they cost a fortune.

"No need," I say. "I will stay here."

ULTIMATELY, the decision gets made for me.

I call home, meaning my parents and brother in New Delhi, with the intent to brainstorm. It's my father who answers. In the thirty seconds it takes for Baba's "hello" to travel from the oval dining table of my childhood and reach the circular dining table I have had since my husband and I got together ten years ago, I break down. I howl, as if fear has ballooned inside me and taken over my entire body and mind. I hear panic in Baba's voice as he frantically calls out to my brother and mother and puts me on speakerphone.

They don't know why I am crying, whether I am emotionally wrecked or in physical pain or both. All they, and I, know is the geographic distance between us.

Right then and there, I make up my mind. I will evacuate to Idaho. I don't need to brainstorm. I know what will happen to my father if I don't try everything I can to keep myself safe. My Baba, who is always strong, who never shows any weakness unless it's my last day during a trip to India and we are hours from when I am supposed to leave for the airport.

I REREAD the property managers' email. I move furniture away from doors and windows. I unplug the TV and return it to its box. I fold clothes and put them away in suitcases. I disconnect everything electronic.

My husband calls to make sure I haven't changed my mind, then adds, just as I am about to hang up, "Don't forget to bring a jacket. It's cold in Idaho."

It doesn't register in my head that everyone everywhere is not in my state of panic. I shake my phone and scream, "No, it's over 80 degrees!"

I look at my belongings, half scattered, half still in boxes. I don't know what to pack, what to squirrel away, what to possibly take to Idaho. My grandfather's memoirs, written at my request in a leather diary? Pictures from my childhood that I have carted around in a thick, brown envelope since my first day in the US in August 2006?

I pace from the bedroom to the kitchen to the study. I prepare my backpack for my flight—medicine kit, granola bars, chewing gum, an extra set of clothes and underwear, Bill Bryson's *I Am a Stranger Here Myself.* I refresh the weather app on my phone. The dense white clot stares right back.

I take off from Wilmington two days before the airport shuts down. I hold my breath until I land in Atlanta, then breathe a bit in Minneapolis, then in Spokane, and then, finally, at home in Moscow. At this point in time, I don't know that Florence will be labeled "a thousand-year storm event" because of the 8 trillion gallons of rain it will pour into North Carolina.

In Moscow, I will revisit the cafés I so missed in Wilmington, but I will be too distracted to read or write. I will refresh my email over and over again, not knowing that campus will remain closed not for a week or two but for a month, something that's never happened in the history of the university despite Wilmington's long tryst with hurricanes.

I won't have known that all over the city, hundreds of trees will fall, in one case killing a mother and her child inside their home. Some neighborhoods will lose everything, and for days Wilmington will remain cut off from the rest of the world, because all roads leading to it will be underwater.

It's only much later that I will learn about the debilitating damage in terms of environmental health. Seven million gallons of waste will spill into the Cape Fear River from hog farms owned by the world's largest pig and pork producer and located in Duplin and Sampson Counties, about an hour north of Wilmington. *Vox* will report the death of 5,500 pigs and 3.4 million chickens. In *Our State* magazine, my colleague Philip Gerard will write about these carcasses finding their way into the Cape Fear River, along with tons and tons of toxic coal ash, plus the breaching of the dam surrounding Sutton Lake—the retention pond that cools water for the local power plant—and about unusual activity at the nuclear power plant in Southport. *A New Yorker* headline will ask, *"Could Smithfield Foods Have Prevented the 'Rivers of Hog Waste' in North Carolina after Florence?"*

In Idaho I will spend time with friends whom I have missed, but I will do so in a state of distraction. I will bristle every time someone will say something like, "What an unexpected vacation for you!" I will think of my students and wonder if everyone made it out, if their homes are okay, if they and their families are safe. For the entire month I will stay in Idaho, I will exist like this, split right down the middle, learning, realizing that sometimes, despite homesickness, you can make yourself a new home in a month.

Back in Wilmington, when the roads clear, a colleague will drive past my apartment building. She will send me pictures of damaged walls, of shingles peeling off the roof. Another colleague will borrow a key from the leasing company, and enter my apartment. She will text, "All is well," and I will want to believe her.

GIRL IN THE RUM BARREL

Searching for a grave is, to some extent, like arranging
to meet a stranger in a café, the lobby of a hotel, or a public square,
in that both activities engender the same way of being there and
looking: at a given distance, every person could be the one waiting for us:
every grave, the one we are searching for.

—VALERIA LUISELLI

WELL INTO THE FIRST SUMMER of the pandemic, my husband and
I, still fairly new residents of coastal North Carolina, decided that
the best thing we could do for ourselves and our marriage was take
day trips to nearby towns. Not only would it give us a better sense
of place, people, and history; it would also give us the chance to try
socially distanced, curbside-pickup local foods. One morning, as we
sat over coffee and toast and planned a future outing, I said, "Maybe
you will see an aspect of North Carolina that you'll realize your life
has needed all along, and you'll love it so much that it'll distract you
from the humidity."

"You mean you're hoping I'll finally stop complaining about whale-mouth weather?" he asked. But at least the ask came with a smile.

FOR DAYS ON END, we had both been unhappy. Stuck inside the four walls of our apartment, we had battled increasing claustrophobia and the screaming matches they seemed to induce: *Do you have to brush your teeth for an hour? Must you nag me about setting the coffee every night? Whose turn is it to load the dishwasher? Why do I have to be the one to clean the bathroom? Why don't you take out the garbage for once? You bought the chicken; you cook it!*

He was unhappy about having had to uproot his life in Idaho for North Carolina and the job and friends he had had to let go, about the greater distance now between us and his parents' home in Los Angeles. I, about the loneliness the pandemic had imposed and the ways my marriage seemed to be unraveling, about how much farther I now felt from my parents in New Delhi, and how terrified I was that COVID-19 would claim them and I would never see them again. Knitted into these feelings was, of course, an overwhelming sense of guilt. How lucky we were that both my husband and I could shelter in place. What exquisite privilege.

I tried to rationalize and then fix my unhappiness. If this pandemic had come when I was a kid, I would have been the happiest person in the world. I would have retreated to my room and made my way through stacks and stacks of books, emerging only for food and bathroom visits. But now everything was different. Everything I had always enjoyed—reading and writing in particular—demanded so much effort.

The reason was simple.

Were it not for the pandemic and its resulting travel restrictions worldwide, I would have been in India, gearing up for my brother's wedding. For months on end, I had been on daily calls with my mother about what to buy, where to buy from, what to gift. I had turned into someone neither I nor my husband recognized.

"You are far more excited for your brother's wedding than you were for ours," he said on numerous occasions, disbelief ringing in his voice.

He was right.

At our wedding, held five years ago on a gorgeous October afternoon, only thirty of our closest people had been in attendance. One of my former professors in Idaho had offered us his home. The ceremony had been in his garden, officiated by one of our best friends. My husband had donned a pink turban, as befitting a Sikh bridegroom. I, on the other hand, had not been a good Hindu bride. I hadn't worn a red sari, opting instead for a bright floral dress bought off of Modcloth. My brother had flown in from India. The day before the wedding, the three of us—my brother, my husband-to-be, and I—had gone flower picking at our nearest U-Pick farm. A friend had baked the dark chocolate ganache and orange marmalade cake. Another had catered the lunch, and our cocktail—a delicious fruity sangria—had been concocted by a clutch of my closest friends. It was different from the kind of wedding my parents might have planned for me. But it was exactly what I wanted for myself. Friends, good food, and plenty of good conversations. What more does one need to start a new chapter of one's life?

By contrast, my brother's wedding was planned as a multicity, weeklong hoopla because our family is split between Delhi and Kolkata. It was supposed to have all the things—gold, silk, marigold flowers, henna, multicourse meals, noisy relatives traveling together from one location to another—that make a solid Indian wedding, and what was more, I was an enthusiastic participant.

When it actually happened, Delhi was under strict lockdown. Invitation cards printed in the hundreds didn't get sent anywhere or to anyone. The two families gathered in the bride's home. All the rituals and festivities were compressed into one day, the bride and groom helped each other get ready, and I watched the ceremony through our dad's phone when he called me on WhatsApp. I held back tears while I was on the call, but for the rest of that day, I was a wreck.

For my own wedding, I had wanted the comfort and companionship of my closest friends. But for my baby brother's wedding, I wanted to shout and scream from the rooftop and have the entire world show up.

The next time a global pandemic occurs, I promise myself, I will be better prepared. I will create a handy, helpful guide on what to do when you can't be with a human being from the outside world for days on end and you must live with your spouse and the inside of your own head.

OUR FIRST TRAVEL DESTINATION in North Carolina—Beaufort—comes highly recommended by one of my colleagues, a long-term resident of the area. "There's a historic cemetery," he says. "You must check it out. They used to offer tours. I don't know if that's still an option."

I look up the cemetery before we set out from home. Pictures show rows upon rows of ancient-looking graves set amid thick, old oaks with armlike branches growing in every possible direction. Located in the historic district of Beaufort, it is called the Old Burying Ground, and it is 300 or so years old. Many of the graves are marked with shell or wood slabs because stone would have been expensive to haul in from afar via ships. As is common in historic seaport towns, some of the graves have vaulted markers covered in brick to protect them from water damage and animals.

I also look up some of the prominent residents of the Old Burying Ground: North Carolina's first naval hero, Captain Otway Burns, and the crew of the *Crissie Wright*, a Philadelphia schooner on its way from Baltimore to Savannah that went aground during a winter storm in January 1886. And a girl who had died at sea and was brought back to North Carolina buried inside a keg of rum.

I AM WHAT ONE might call a casual tapophile, a person interested in cemeteries and gravestones. Other terms include "graver" or "tomb tourist," the latter having been popularized by author Scott Stanton. I imagine my confession takes away some of my good Hindu points, should any of our gods and goddesses be distributing them at any time, as I imagine mine is not the most popular pastime, given that we cremate our dead. I remember as a fourteen-year-old vacationing with my family in the Himalayan cities of Dharamsala and Palampur, and my favored places to check out on that trip had not been ancient temples dedicated to gods and goddesses, but "modern," barely 200-year-old cemeteries full of British officers and ladies, their last resting spots offering them magnificent views of the mountains towering on all sides. I want to credit my parents for putting up with such requests and not smothering me with the kind of admonitions that are, I imagine, reserved for children and young people in more traditional Hindu households: *do not visit cemeteries, do not visit cemeteries especially after dark; however, if you must, shower as soon as you return home.*

No ancestor of mine is buried anywhere, so I am not sure I know or understand the roots of my fascination. Perhaps I like cemeteries because I don't associate them with loss, because though I have lost beloved family members and friends, I have never witnessed a burial. I wonder if my subconscious thinks it's something that happens in books and movies. It's something that happens to other people.

Or perhaps I like cemeteries for their peace and quiet. Hindu cremation sites, at least in my experience, can be noisy, chaotic places, bereft of the kind of solitude and space, both physical as well as personal, one might seek when raw with grief. On the other hand, cemeteries, at least the ones I have visited thus far, seem to offer both the space and atmosphere one needs for quiet contemplation.

Perhaps the most obvious reason I like cemeteries is that I like history and storytelling. I especially like stories that exist outside official, documented records. At museums and historic sites, I am less interested in the person whose portrait hangs on the wall or whose bust commemorates which treaty was signed, when, and where.

Instead, I am far more curious about everything that happened behind the scenes. Who made the breakfasts that allowed them to be so great? After all, it's challenging, if not impossible, to reach one's full potential if one is also battling, say, poverty, or an empty stomach. And who washed their clothes to make them appear so dapper in public? Who cut their hair and or maintained their wigs? Who offered a patient ear and wise counsel? Who had no choice *but* to offer a patient ear and wise counsel?

Perhaps my love for graves also speaks to my love for stories about treasure hunts and mysteries. As a kid, I spent many afternoons drawing elaborate maps and trails on the floor of our balcony. My school-bus best friend—different from my neighborhood best friend and my classroom best friend—and I invented a language, replete with its own unique script. When I was twelve, my then pen friend and I wrote to each other using a code of our own creation. When my brother was a baby and a fussy eater, I often helped our mother feed him by telling him stories I made up on the spot about mysterious places, evil villains, alien life-forms, and heroes and heroines on quests.

When I walk past graves and read people's names and dates, I can't help but think that just moments ago, all these people were alive and going about their daily business. They were doing exactly or reasonably exactly the things I do now—reach out to friends, worry about parents, assemble sandwiches for lunch, fold clothes, gossip with the spouse, stand in line behind the slowest person in the grocery store, forget birthdays, and so on and so forth.

Sure, their voices have gone quiet now. As have their headaches of class, gender, dreams, health, and wealth. No words can wound them, no jabs can shred their egos. No Instagram post can remind them to set time aside on Sundays for self-care. Nor can they tell me what leaps of imagination I can or cannot make based on how I interpret their epitaphs.

Who else were they besides their names and dates and the kind of sentimentality we typically reserve for those who lived in times before ours? Why do we assume—naively, stupidly—that somehow their lives were simpler, less complex than ours?

IN OLDER CEMETERIES, when the epitaph is wordy and detailed, it is almost always for a man who lived a long and distinguished life. In my head, such men are white and wrinkled, with icy blue eyes, thin lips, sunken cheeks, and bearing the disapproving expressions of British colonizers in India captured for eternity in sepia photographs. You can see them too, can't you? Seated on wooden chairs, their backs straight, faces unsmiling, their heads protected from the savage Indian sun by pith helmets, the camera having caught them with their latest conquests, rows and rows of dead, just-hunted tigers arranged like pillows at their feet. Despite what they did to those tigers, the men were so dear to their families that they were honored with the most impressive resting places available. Hence the elaborate grave, the detailed epitaph. Or perhaps it's because the dearly departed's will said, *If I don't get an over-the-top funeral, you don't get a cent.*

By contrast, when the epitaph says something like "beloved daughter" or "virtuous mother," I imagine the woman in the mold of Beth March. She is good and kind-hearted, perhaps the owner of a few stylish bonnets and lace handkerchiefs, but unlike her sister Jo, she is not the heroine of her life or story.

Or perhaps the real reason I like cemeteries is envy. Or longing. Or a combination of the two. Maybe it's resentment that there is nowhere on earth I can go and "be" with any of my grandmothers or great-grandmothers. Sure, there would have been no two-way conversation, no secrets exchanged in hushed whispers about random family members, nor disagreements over what kind of tea goes best with what kind of biscuits.

But how might it have felt to see these women's names being given some semblance of permanence? Would I have brought flowers for them? Lit candles at the foot of their graves? I don't know. But I can imagine the one-sided conversation I would have carried on, mostly in the form of questions. *Did it make a difference in your own life when India won freedom? Or did you feel left out of the conversation because the men who signed these documents did so from far away, unaware of you and your reality? Did you ever want to travel? Did you ever not want to be a mother? Would you have opted to marry late, say at thirty-five, if you had the option?*

UNLIKE ME, my husband is not a fan of cemeteries. As a Sikh, his faith too, like mine, demands cremation and not burial as the final rite of passage. But I don't think his ambivalence toward cemeteries has anything to do with Sikhism, just like my fascination has nothing to do with Hinduism per se. All I know is that he doesn't care for them. On various trips, I have suggested walks to local cemeteries, and he has said no, even when we have been in towns as historic and interesting as Point Arena in California. I wonder if, despite his fondness for history, he finds walking through crumbling graves a pointless exercise. Too much work for too little payoff.

On our way to Beaufort, however, he agrees to explore the Old Burial Grounds with me. Surely this, I think to myself as I slide into the passenger seat of our Subaru, is one positive outcome of the pandemic.

BEAUFORT IS A TOWN of many charms. Established in 1713, it is the fourth-oldest town in North Carolina. Thus far, its most famous resident has been Blackbeard, who ran the *Queen Anne's Revenge*, his pirate flagship, to the ground. Today Beaufort is a tourist magnet replete with nautical-themed gift shops, overpriced bed and breakfasts, and lots of surfers.

Inside the Old Burying Ground, there are no physical maps to be found anywhere. My husband downloads a map and a walking tour app on his phone. He puts it on speaker and raises the volume so we can hear the guide over the loud calls of a particularly energetic mockingbird.

Most of the graves are covered with moss and their epitaphs barely legible. The once clearly etched angels have faded. As have the words, flowers, and leaves. Only their shadows linger. The ground is littered with dead leaves and overgrown grass. Several gravestones have tilted to one side. The damp North Carolina soil has no mercy. The trees are so lush and huge, they are straight out of the kinds of fairy tales I loved as a kid, and there are areas of the grounds that have clearly not seen any sunshine in years.

Since arriving in North Carolina in 2018, here's my one true observation about the trees in this fine state. They are majestic in a grave, sepulchral way. They are not here to make friends. They are not here to amuse you or play with you. Each tree here carries an entire universe onto itself. Seemingly, they grow out of each other, entwined like lovers or cramped like a family of twenty sheltering under the same dinky roof during a thunderstorm.

Ferns spiral out of branches and sub-branches. The kind that's known as resurrection fern lives on large trees, usually oaks. Coarse to the touch, it curls up its fronds and *dies* when it hasn't rained for a while. But it reappears, *resurrects*, at the first sign of rain, eager to show off its carpeting skills. Then there is Spanish moss, which until you have seen it or touched it seems like the most ethereal of creations. It falls from branches like curtains in the most gothic of mansions.

MINUTES INTO THE TOUR, sweat pools on our foreheads and pours down our faces. Still, this is our first proper outing since the pandemic upended our lives, and neither of us will be the first to suggest we return to Wilmington and the air-conditioned comfort of our apartment.

It also helps that we are not the only ones here, although we might be the only ones religiously following the directions of our electronic guide. Scattered through the grounds are couples like us, and a few groups of college-age friends. A family of four is closest to us: a mom, a dad, and two daughters, who look to be around eight and ten, respectively. All four of them are dressed in shorts. The girls have matching white T-shirts. The younger one, in particular, seems to be in a good mood. She keeps rushing from one numerical marker to the next. This is clearly a treasure hunt for her. She will follow all the clues to the proverbial pot of gold—untold riches and rewards— that are no doubt waiting for her at the end of this ambitious quest.

I call out to "Mom." "Do you know what kind of tree this is?" I ask, my finger pointing at yet another impressive specimen.

"No idea," she says with a shrug. She repeats my question to her partner, who replies with a touch of surety in his voice, "Hemlock, I think."

Suddenly a blond boy of about five shoots out from behind the trees and aims, seemingly, straight for me. He is dressed in all white, and his mop of hair is so pale it looks unreal. Turns out, he is the youngest child of this family. He skips ahead to join his sisters.

My husband and I exchange glances. I purse my mouth so I can suppress my giggle. I know he knows exactly what sprang to my mind when the little, pale boy bolted into view. We have watched way too many terrible movies about haunted houses and child ghosts, especially ones with hair like that.

We follow the instructions of our electronic guide and make it to the other side of the Old Burial Ground, where a simple wooden gravestone says, "Little Girl Buried." While none of the other graves had any offerings on them besides the odd candle or fake flower, this small grave, no bigger than four feet by two feet, has been overtaken by gifts. Teddy bears that were once bright and cheerful, but the unforgiving weather has rendered them scruffy and discolored. Ornate shells. Painted rocks, plastic flowers, ribbons, frilly bows, and a plethora of toys—cars, dolls, coins, pens, pictures of Winnie the Pooh. I even spot a wide-toothed black comb.

My mind goes back to what I had read about this little girl. She was only six years old, and eager to see England. Her father was not opposed to the idea, but her mother was reluctant to let her travel so far. Finally she relented, but only because her husband promised that no matter what happened, he would bring their daughter home safely.

Father and daughter set sail. They reached England and had a jolly good time. On their way back to North Carolina, though, the girl contracted an unexpected illness. She died at sea. Her father, however, kept his promise. Instead of burying her at sea, as was the norm those days, he purchased a keg of rum instead and placed her in it so she would be preserved in the alcohol. Once they reached home, he buried his daughter here, in the Old Burial Ground in Beaufort.

I want to know why the girl wanted to visit England so desperately. After she died, how many times must her poor mother have asked herself the same question? And how many times must her father have regretted his decision? What pot of gold was she looking for in England? An audience with the queen? I imagine her reason was the same as for any of us who like to travel: a little bit of adventure, a change from our daily lives and routine, the chance to eat and drink new things, meet people who don't make up our everyday existence, breathe in air that's different—not necessarily better or worse, just different.

I also want to know more about the people who treat her grave as a pilgrimage site. Why do they come here? What do they gain by leaving offerings? Comfort, perhaps. Or hope. If she made it back home, so might those they are searching for.

A FEW STEPS FROM the Old Burial Ground sits the most picturesque part of downtown Beaufort. The waterfront streets spill over with restaurants, ice cream stores, and shops selling both charming and kitschy knickknacks, the mainstay of any tourist-friendly town.

We walk into one selling all kinds of local goodies and handicrafts. I grab a basket and hungrily start putting items in it—muscadine jelly, strawberry and walnut jam, a bottle of spicy blueberry glaze, tomatillo salsa, a sample pack of grits, a one-pound bag of the prettiest beans I have ever seen. Uncooked, they are about the same size as black beans, and each kernel looks like someone carefully, attentively hand-painted abstract designs in red, pink, brown, and beige. I learn later they are called borlotti beans or cranberry beans, a staple in Italian and Portuguese cooking.

After much deliberation, I toss in a final item—a pair of inch-long earrings. They are made of some kind of light wood, and the artist has painted brightly colored fish on them.

As I pay for my items, the lady behind the counter points at our masks and says, "Take them off, I tell ya. I used to be a doctor, you know. There is nothing called COVID."

I look deeply into her eyes visible over her own mask—I am glad the mask mandate is in place—to see if she is joking. Next to me, I sense my husband shift on his feet. Though I don't turn around to check, I imagine the horror in his eyes matches mine. Does the woman notice it too? Does she think we are so sheeplike that in addition to following rules about masking, we have trained even our expressions to match?

She continues without needing any prompting or encouragement from us. "Believe me. There really is nothing called COVID. It's a government conspiracy." She waves a dismissive hand, whether at the government or at us, the dumb tourists who follow such mandates, I am not sure.

As we leave the store, I am overtaken by regret, the kind I have never experienced before, especially not after purchasing a delightful piece of jewelry and bags full of delicious treats. Fifty percent of my brain wants to return to the store and challenge her; the other 50 percent has seen too many videos of people believing this virus is a hoax and, worse, pulling down the masks of others. Plus, in America I always, always live with the fear that the person in front of me or behind me or anywhere around me could be carrying a gun and that any action of mine could provoke them to pull it out.

I force myself to think cheerful thoughts. This, right here, is another reason we travel, isn't it? This is why we leave the safety and comfort of our homes, why we cross oceans, why we traipse through graveyards, sweaty and exhausted, during a global pandemic? So we can feel a little out of sorts. So we can be reminded that we will never know with certainty what to expect and that losing control over our tightly orchestrated daily lives is not always a terrible thing.

But then, this, right here, is also why we marry. Why we seek a mate who more or less fits our vision of who we want to be, who we know we are not, and what our present and future should look like. This is why we attend parties and engage with others outside our specific domestic bubbles. So that once we are back home, we have an ally with whom to dissect other people and their weirdness.

I had found the pot of gold—the rewards and riches—that marked the purpose of our outing to Beaufort: from the exquisite beauty of the cemetery, the macabre experience of the little girl's grave, the unexpected conversation with the COVID denier, to the peace and quiet with my husband for one whole day. So I did what would be the right thing to do at the end of a treasure quest. I grabbed my husband's hand, and together we went off in search of food.

IN CASE OF AN
ACTIVE SHOOTER

IDENTIFY YOUR LOCATION

A nondescript classroom in the building that houses your department. One door. Three large windows. A writing board with markers passed down from one semester to the next. A digital console and all the technology you will need to project your lesson or stream from YouTube.

Nineteen students. Plus you, their instructor. You all have rearranged the chairs and desks to form a loose rectangle so you can see each other and your respective laptops.

This classroom is located at one end of the building. It's conveniently close to the toilets and water fountain, and to one of the many doors left unlocked during the workday so anyone may enter or exit without any delay.

Like other buildings on this campus, this one has redbrick walls outside and thumbtacked posters and announcements on noticeboards inside. Paths that lead to and from here are lined with thick oaks, from whose branches Spanish moss hangs like bracelets. Several trees fell during Hurricane Florence last year. You wouldn't know it, though, unless someone told you and or showed you the signs.

Like other American universities, this one, where you teach, is large and tidy; interspersed with convenient benches and food courts every few feet; and chaotically busy during the day with cars, bikes, skateboards, and pedestrians. Because this is also the South, you can skip the benches and choose to sit on swings and rocking chairs instead. They are on nearly every porch. In fact, even the local airport has white rocking chairs, right next to the baggage claim area. As if, while waiting for your bags to arrive, you might want to snooze a little, take in the view, chat with your neighbor over sweet iced tea.

In the evenings, the campus might as well be dead. On your fifteen-minute walk back home, you rarely see more than five people. You send pictures of vivid sunsets and dreamy Spanish moss to your mother in New Delhi, and she asks, "Where is everyone?"

In theory, though, the classroom in which you are teaching could be any classroom, in any school, college, or university, anywhere in the United States. Just like in the movies. Especially the American movies and television shows you watched when you were a kid in India. How you longed for a campus exactly like the one in *Beverly Hills 90210*. So many colors and joys. So much freedom! The kids there didn't have to wear uniforms, unlike the suffering you and everyone else at your school had to endure. There they could date openly, stay out until midnight, sometimes even longer, and they still didn't get into trouble with their parents. They could wear lipstick and nail polish. Whereas if you attempted either in view of the Catholic nuns who ran your school, there would be serious consequences.

What never occurred to you all those years ago, when you devoured episodes of *Beverly Hills 90210* as if they were divine offerings blessed by the gods, was that one day you could very well end up on such a campus. First, as a student. And then, a few years later, as a professor. And that one day, right in the middle of class, your laptop screen could turn green, with bright red capital letters flashing six words on repeat: "Active Shooter Alert. Seek Immediate Shelter."

DOES THIS ROOM HAVE AN INTERCOM?

When you read this question on the "In Case of an Active Shooter" poster placed inside the classroom, it occurs to you that neither you as the professor nor any of your nineteen students have probably had to think about intercoms thus far this semester. You wonder if any of them even knows what an intercom is.

You do, because in the Hindi movies you watched as a kid, the villain, usually fabulously wealthy and in possession of a powerful voice and mustache, had multiple phones on his desk. He would reach for one after another to instruct his associates, threaten rivals, intimidate honest police officers, hobnob with corrupt politicians, and whisper sweet nothings to his moll waiting upstairs.

But that was in the late 1980s. Maybe even in the early 1990s. This is nearly thirty years later, with iPhones in every hand. When, where, how, and why are you or anyone else supposed to think of intercoms?

KNOW that when your laptop starts flashing green, your first instinct will be to panic. Is that a malicious virus downloading itself automatically? But then you will read the words, as will all your students on their respective laptops. Six words on repeat: "Active Shooter Alert. Seek Immediate Shelter."

This course you have been entrusted to teach your nineteen students is titled Issues of Diversity in Publishing. In the overall scheme of things, such as subjects on which you are somewhat of an expert and why you were hired by this department in the first place, these issues matter. It's important that your students know, and care about, who published whom; whose works are taught in classrooms ranging from elementary to high school and beyond; whose books are arranged in eye-catching displays inside stores and libraries; whose works are reviewed in the *New York Times*; what the numbers and averages are inside the publishing industry; who are the gatekeepers; who wrote an article about said gatekeepers in last year's trendiest magazine; who popularized that article through a new hashtag; and who all changed their profile pictures to reflect their solidarity and bleeding hearts.

But in the larger scheme of things—such as life and death—a semester-long course on diversity in publishing matters as much as pearls to a swine. What matters is that suddenly you, with your MFA degree in creative nonfiction and your knowledge of narrative arcs and how to write good scenes and dialogue, are in charge of nineteen lives. Twenty if you count your own.

RUN to fish out your cell phone from your bag. Watch your students do the same. They dig into their jackets and jeans, backpacks, and pencil bags. Why is yours buried under receipts? Why do you have so many keys? A pocket mirror and lipsticks? Why do you have them? Why have you ever needed them?

When you find your phone, text your husband. Everyone else you love to the same obscene degree—your parents and your brother— are far away in India. It's 12:30 p.m. here on the East Coast, so it's 2 a.m. in India. Your eyes glaze over as you try to make sense of words. What do you type? What do you tell your husband? Are you supposed to sound profound? Funny? Loving? How do you sum up ten years of a life with someone in one text?

You don't know. Though you have been writing since you were six years old and teaching creative writing for almost twelve years to the day, and you have supported every iteration of the iPhone, it's like you have neither seen nor touched this keyboard before.

HIDE yourself and your nineteen students. Hide under desks that are made of plastic and have wheels on them so the lightweight furniture can be easily rearranged to suit the nature of instruction the professor wants to impart. If it's a workshop, sit in a circle. If it's a lecture, a semicircle might be better.

The classroom has that one door, with a slim glass panel built right in the middle of it. You can both look out into the corridor outside and be looked at by someone standing in that corridor. Across from the door, there are three generous-sized windows. They offer gorgeous views of other redbrick buildings with arched windows, and that Spanish moss you can't get enough of.

You consider the windows. You feel something like hope, intense and glowing like the red cardinals on every tree of this campus, until you remember an email exchange from a previous semester wherein you learned that all windows of the building are sealed and cannot be opened.

FIGHT to stay rooted where you are. Watch, as if through a haze, as if time has stopped, as your students send texts or whisper-call their parents, partners, best friends, and roommates, as a few of them break down on each other's shoulders, as others reach to comfort them, offer hugs, and hold hands.

Last year, when you attended the weeklong New Faculty Orientation, a Safety Workshop was offered on the first day. At the start of the hour, when the instructor said, "Step one: remain calm," the audience responded with nervous laughter. Each of the seventy-odd new faculty, including you, was reminded that your degrees weren't enough. That you knew how to teach was not enough. You had to be a warrior as well, a condition of employment in this and other beautiful campuses of America that you might see in the movies.

After that workshop, on your way back home, you had counted your credentials: maker of decent sandwiches and soups; competent doer of dishes and sweeper of floors; reluctant doer of laundry; enthusiastic reader, writer, and teacher of books; fairly reliable and trustworthy friend; could-be-better wife, daughter, and sister.

But as a warrior? A big, fat, incompetent zero. You have never even fired a gun, though friends and colleagues have offered to teach you. Even though you are far from timid. Or so you believe, because you regularly watch horror movies for fun, because you have lived in many cities and held different jobs. Even though one time when you were out for dinner with five of your favorite former students, the discussion revealed that among them they owned thirty-six guns.

Stunned, you had watched their faces—young and white, ranging between the ages of twenty and twenty-two—as they exchanged notes on makes and other specifics. Their guns had come to them in the form of birthday presents. Graduation gifts. As inheritances and loans.

Perhaps, deep down, it all boils down to one simple fact: in the India where you were born and raised, the India where you lived the first twenty-seven years of your life before you came to America, you knew that only two kinds of people owned and used guns—cops and bad guys—and you were/are neither.

One incident in particular burns in your memory. The year was 1999, and you were twenty years old, a student in Delhi, living at home. On April 30, a young woman named Jessica Lal was shot dead in your city. She was a model, a minor celebrity of sorts. On the night she was murdered, Jessica was working at a glitzy bar owned by yet another celebrity. Their liquor license prohibited them from selling alcoholic drinks after 12:30 a.m. And so, shortly after 12:30 a.m., when a young man named Manu Sharma approached the bar, Jessica refused.

Manu offered her money. Jessica refused again. Manu pulled out a pistol and fired a warning shot into the ceiling. Still, Jessica could not be intimidated. Manu aimed his pistol again, this time straight at Jessica. When he fired, the bullet struck her in the head, killing Jessica instantly.

You and the entire city woke up to this news the next morning. For days on end, no one talked of anything else. Of course, violent crimes and murders weren't unheard-of in Delhi. It is an old, complex, complicated city after all. It's the capital of the country, the seat of power, home to more than 15 million residents. People have killed and died here for the same reasons they have killed and died in other places: love, land, money, power, gods, and everything else that can be coveted, disputed, or avenged.

But the horror of Jessica's murder felt different. Perhaps it was the casual nature of it. The realization that Jessica could have been anyone. A friend, a neighbor, a senior in college. Or you. That her life had mattered so little to her murderer that in one fell swoop he decimated the building blocks that made her who she was—her family, work, friendships.

Manu, Jessica's murderer, looked like a normal person too. Like someone you might run into while buying bread or waiting for the bus. Not a Hindi-movie villain from the 1980s. Not an old, corrupt politician or a power-hungry policeman. So why did he own a gun?

Why did he take it to the bar? The questions were endless because it was unthinkable that a regular young person could own a gun, carry it about on their person, threaten another regular young person, and kill over something as unremarkable as a drink.

Surely something like this happened only in lawless lands run by thugs. The kind you saw in action movies. Or in news reports of countries in shambles. Where angry, bitter men operating in mobs filled up your television screen. Armed to the teeth, they puffed their chests, drove military vehicles marked with their flags and insignia, and charged into government buildings.

BACK IN YOUR CLASSROOM, you don't know the identity of the gunman. But in your imagination you give him a face, a body. You think he might be young. Between twenty and twenty-five years old. A loner, possibly, with an arsenal of guns and bullets stashed in his room. What was he out to avenge? A professor who didn't give a generous grade? A friend who betrayed? A romantic partner who walked away? Or just because?

HOW TO RESPOND WHEN LAW ENFORCEMENT ARRIVES or, as in this case, when you don't exactly remember how the next few minutes unfold. Did an "All clear" message flash on your screens? Or did your nineteen students and you simply walk out of the classroom when it felt safe?

Quietly but quickly, you went to your office on the other end of the building. You locked your door and dropped into your chair. You called your husband when you were able to. You told your parents three years later.

WHEN YOU LOOKED UP the total number of mass shootings for 2019, you learned that it was 435, 111 more than in 2018. In 2020, that number jumped to 614, and in 2021, to 693. You also learned that there isn't a uniform, agreed-on definition of what qualifies as mass shootings. The one that makes the most sense to you is from *Mother Jones*: "any event where three or more people are shot and killed in a public place."

That day in the classroom, you didn't know that a worldwide pandemic was just around the corner. That working from home was about to become the norm, and Zoom, or "new Skype," everyone's best friend, colleague, friend, and family.

You didn't know that you wouldn't be able to go home to India for three years. That every day, your social media feed will fill up with losses. That you'd miss your brother's wedding, stay put in your southern city, and order groceries, lipstick, and nail polish through screens. That on days when you and your husband were exhausted by each other's company, you'd miss your large, sprawling campus, its red cardinals and Spanish moss, even those swings and rocking chairs, and especially your big-hearted students who looked out for each other.

Day after day, you will watch the news with disbelief at armed protesters puffing their chests, marching against masks and vaccines, and mobs storming government buildings. You will stare at their body armor, at their vehicles, at the number of guns at their disposal, and you will wonder how regular people can afford specialized, expensive gear like this. You will try looking for answers, even more so for your mother, who will ask from India, "Why does everything need to be protested with guns?"

In time you will tire of screens and Zoom. But because they will allow you to teach from your desk at home—and by "teach," I mean all those things like narrative arcs, scenes, and dialogue, things you know and have trained for—you will feel grateful. You will remember, often, in fact every time you hear of a gunman somewhere, that neither you nor your nineteen students became a statistic in 2019. You will try to forgive yourself for not being a warrior.

A CAFÉ OF ONE'S OWN

ON A SATURDAY MORNING, sometime in mid-August 2006, I stepped inside an American café for the very first time. I had won a ten-dollar gift certificate in a drawing held during the weeklong international students' orientation. For me, an impoverished student, ten dollars was a princely amount. Barely a week ago, I had arrived from New Delhi to enroll as a graduate student of creative writing at the University of Idaho. All I had were my savings from four years of working as an editor and a loan from a friend, which amounted to just enough to keep me afloat for one semester. Because ours was a three-year program, the remaining five semesters loomed before me, frightening and unknown. What gave me hope, and tenacity, was my urge to learn how to write, and my fantastic roommate, Manasi. She was on her way to getting a PhD in biology and also happened to be from India.

That first time I stepped inside Moscow's One World Café, Manasi was my much-needed guide. Someone had to hold my hand as I stared at a menu board chalk-marked with unfamiliar and confusing drink options. *What is a latte? How is an Americano different from an espresso?* Back then, Starbucks and other such chains had yet to make their mark in India. Now, of course, you can't walk in any Indian city without running into a café selling everything from mochas to cappuccinos to that monstrosity known unironically as chai latte containing ingredients such as maple syrup and vanilla extract. *Either commit to a chai or to a coffee, people. What kind of daily indecisiveness do you battle that you must find ways to marry the two?*

Inside One World Café, I was taken in by its high ceilings, with the exposed pipes and woodwork, the red brick and orange walls, the comfortable if mismatched chairs, the glass tabletops with maps carved out of wood and set against oceans made of coffee beans, and the doors to nowhere that hung from various heights.

It's been a little over fifteen years since that day, and I don't remember my precise order anymore. I am guessing it was a mocha and a sandwich. But I remember that Manasi and I sat at a table by the windows. There was music playing in the background, but also the telltale sounds of the industrial-sized coffee grinder, the hiss of steam and pour of beverage, the dinging of the cash register, and the back-and-forth between the customers and the baristas. Manasi and I chatted. We worked on our respective homework, and every now and then I stared out of the huge windows to make sense of this new world where I had just arrived.

I was homesick. I was nervous. And I felt very rootless. How was I going to survive the next three years of my MFA? How would I pay rent? Or buy groceries? What, if any, jobs would I get here, given the number of restrictions put in place for foreign students?

Yet there was much to be grateful for: the hilly, leafy campus of the University of Idaho; the English department housed inside a historic building full of strange passageways and apparently a ghost or two; the professors and peers who had been so welcoming; the variety of classes I was taking, ranging from Jewish American Literature to Workshops in Fiction; the red-roofed apartment Manasi and I lived in from which both the campus and downtown were comfortable walks away; the cold, crisp northern Idaho weather; my new friends Parul and Leslie, who had taken me to Walmart and Ross so I could buy a floor mattress and weather-appropriate clothes; and Manasi herself. There were only a handful of things I had known about her before we signed our lease. Now, in this one week, I had learned a lot more: she cooked great food, she laughed at my bad jokes, she shared my love for Hindi movies, and she generously loaned me her phone and her laptop so I could be in touch with my family, because I had no money for either.

And now, here was One World Café to add to my list of "Things to Be Grateful For." I hadn't known anything like this when I was growing up in New Delhi. Sure, there were plenty of restaurants, and cafés too, but you went to them with friends or family or colleagues, or if you were on a date. There were few public places that I, a young woman, had been able to claim for myself, where I could remain uninterrupted and undisturbed and just drink coffee, do homework, and stare out of the window.

Even now, after so many years, I still don't think I have the words to adequately explain what it meant to suddenly have this gift of space. To be able to step out of my red-roofed apartment in Idaho's late summer / early fall weather, walk the twenty minutes to downtown Moscow without having to hear a single catcall, and enter this light-filled, fresh-brewed, coffee-scented world.

Overnight, One World became my refuge, albeit an expensive one, even after I landed two on-campus jobs: as a student mentor and a writing center tutor. So I stopped spending money on pretty much everything else. This was a habit I had to sustain. It was enough that I could be in something so filled with music, charm, and local life. That I could do it by myself, and whenever I felt like it, without needing the crutch of a friend or a companion, made it that much more special.

Soon fall turned to winter, the kind of winter I had never experienced before. The freezing air clawed my face, the slippery ice made me cry out more than once in fear and frustration, and my gloves from Ross Dress for Less did not offer enough protection. My brown knuckles turned black, and when I went to the doctor, she said, "Your skin isn't used to this. It's protesting this cold. You have to keep your hands moisturized all the time." That first winter in Idaho, when I still had no way to know how I would pay for the next two years of the program, when everything outside was cloudy, snowy, and seeped in homesickness, the warmth and light inside One World made a huge difference. I went to it every day as soon as I got done with my classes. Sometimes I went with friends, and over mugs of delicious coffee we wrote, we complained, we read each other's words, and we commiserated.

As in any good story, in my case, too, things did fall into place eventually. I won scholarships and completed my program. Where once I was a student, now I became a lecturer, and despite having an office on campus, One World Café became my other, more favored office. It's where I went to read, prepare lectures, grade papers, and design syllabi for upcoming courses. It's where I met with colleagues and students. And it continued to be my favorite place to meet friends, write, and people-watch and eavesdrop—foundational habits for any writer.

We don't realize how much a place becomes us until we leave it behind. Back in 2006, when I left India for Idaho, I yearned for some of its places the same way I yearned for my friends and family. I struggled to find options that could fill the void created in the absence of my mother's bedroom, her kitchen, and the balcony adjoining her bedroom, where she and I would talk for hours at length. Or the food stand, where my father and I would stop for tea and spicy omelets on our way back home from our respective offices. Or the movie theater I would most often visit with my brother, or the famed restaurant Karim's in Old Delhi—established in 1913 by chefs who had once worked in the royal Mughal kitchens—that my friends and I frequented for their soft, pillowy sheermal and slow-cooked mutton korma.

These days, I live 2,800 miles away in North Carolina in a city by the Atlantic Ocean. Every day, I am grateful for the job that's brought me here, for the bleached finds I bring home from the beach, and for the red cardinals that live on the campus where I teach.

Yet there are mornings when I wake up with an acute longing for that café I left behind in Moscow. Sleepily, I shake my husband's shoulder and murmur, "I will go down to One World and finish the story I have been working on. Join me when you can?" The next instant, I will remember where I am. I will pull my hand away and let him sleep. I too will remain in bed for a few extra minutes, my eyes squeezed shut, the covers up to my chin, and "walk" to One World as I used to from our last apartment, the one right in downtown, a mere seven-minute stroll away.

Inside, I will "see" all the usual suspects. The owner of a beloved restaurant backslapping the friend of a friend, who has just started his photography business. There, by the water tap, my favorite student from two years ago talking to one of my current students, who is here to do her homework. At the table closest to the door, the man who once tried to convert me to his very specific brand of Christianity, and at the table diagonally across from him, the friendly lady with green hair and a shoulder bag with the picture of a bird on it. In the back room, a group has gathered around the big table, and together they are figuring out the schedule for the upcoming music festival. They remind me of the summer I reserved that room for a course I was teaching for the first time. I had titled it Conflict Fiction from South Asia. I remember students telling me how much they loved being here as opposed to our regular classroom, and what a treat it was to reward oneself with a coffee or a cookie while discussing issues as weighty as independence and Partition.

I open my eyes. I bring myself back to my current reality. If I keep my eyes closed any longer, I will linger, and one by one I will see even more of the usual suspects—current and former grad students from the program I was in, my professors who later became my colleagues, neighbors I never got a chance to catch up with in the building we shared, but inside the café we all seemed to have time for a wave and a "Hey, how's it going?" I sift through my memories—hundreds, no, thousands of them that are bound to this café. Of friends sharing news of their loves; of breaking down over loss and betrayal; of farewells to friends like Manasi, Parul, and Leslie, who left Moscow years before I did. Of early dates over coffee with my then-boyfriend and now-husband, and the art installations, music concerts, and readings, including mine, that the café hosted and we attended over the years. Not to mention the months he worked there himself, as a barista, and I felt ridiculously spoiled every time a specially concocted beverage landed at my table.

Fifteen years ago, when Manasi helped me use my gift certificate, I could not have anticipated that a café would come to signify everything positive I associate with the life I have built for myself in America—the warmth of strangers, the freedom to occupy public spaces, the right to feel safe, the intersection of community and friendship, the comfort of being seen out and about in the world by myself, and, of course, delicious coffee. I will keep those memories and content myself in this new city of mine, where I will seek a substitute.

Soon, soon.

CHOCOLATE-MARMALADE
GREEN CARD

MY HUSBAND AND I got summoned for my green card interview on April 6, 2016. We had been expecting it. Correction: we had been wanting it. An interview meant that the application he had submitted back in December 2015 had cleared its first hurdle. He had spent months on it—organizing and cataloguing documents including receipts of items purchased together; photographs of us clicked by others and ourselves showing the passage of time; postcards we had happened to exchange anytime we had lived long distance; forms detailing everything from my medical to academic to employment history; letters of support from our respective employers, friends, and former professors wherein they vouched for how long they had known us (individually and as a couple), in what capacity, and that we were/are indeed stellar specimens of humanity.

I also had to undergo a full health evaluation and attach relevant documents as proof. But I couldn't just go to my regular doctor. That was not an option, though I had been her patient for the last five years. No, I had to go to one specifically designated for immigration purposes. He was an older gentleman, old enough to be my grandfather, and his clinic was forty-five miles from our then-hometown of Moscow, Idaho. To be fair, the doctor was a thorough professional. During the breast examination portion, a female nurse remained present in the room. Every second of their insistent prodding, I reminded myself to stay pleasant, smile, and not show any outward signs of discomfort, because I needed their approval to be able to live with my own husband.

In the end, the total number of pages for the application came close to 350, the size of a full-length manuscript, a book on which rested our futures.

THE EVENING BEFORE the interview—April 5—my husband and I made the two-hour drive from our home to Spokane, Washington. We checked into a hotel a short distance from where we were going to be interviewed the following afternoon. We were well acquainted with Spokane. We came here often. On weekend getaways, or anytime Moscow's familiarity and small-town-ness got to us. For two people raised in New Delhi and Los Angeles respectively, Spokane scratched a little of the itch we felt, that craving for the big city, where you can lose yourself in a downtown where no one knows you, and you are just another face, anonymous, unremarkable, unworthy of a second glance.

But this was not like those trips. There was too much at stake. Too much. We had told my family in Delhi the purpose behind our trip. No one else. The alternative to my not getting the green card seemed too much to even contemplate. A marriage split between countries and continents. *Surely*, we consoled ourselves, *it wouldn't be so bad.* There were numerous couples who had it much, much worse. What if one of us had been in the army, deployed somewhere dangerous? This was fine. This we could manage. I would return to Delhi, get a job, live at my parents' home for a while. We could travel between India and the US during the holidays. We could chat via WhatsApp, send heart emojis on Facebook Messenger, give each other sloppy kisses over Facetime.

By then we had been together for eight years, albeit married for less than six months. We had survived serious health scares and nights stretched taut with concerns over jobs and money. Surely we could manage an interview.

INSIDE THE HOTEL ROOM, I turned on the giant TV. My husband ordered us pizzas. I hated it even though there was nothing wrong with the order. I sobbed into my slice. He chewed slowly, knowing full well it wasn't the pizza that had got me upset.

Neither of us slept that night. We had read horror stories about couples being interviewed separately just to see if their answers matched. There was no room for error or forgetfulness. All questions were apparently fair questions. We could be asked anything, so long as it covered our married life, whether in the bedroom or at the dining table.

We held hands. I fiddled with his kara, the thick iron bangle he wears on his right wrist. The kara is one of five articles of faith for Sikhs and they are never to take it off as its purpose is to remind them to be good, to do God's work. My husband is not a religious man but his kara means a great deal to him. It belonged to his late grandfather, an army man, who fought in World War II for the British Indian Army, and later for the Indian Army in India's wars against Pakistan in 1965 and 1971. In all the time we have been together, he has taken his kara off only twice. Once, for a TSA agent at the airport in Las Vegas who refused to let him through without examining the kara, and the second time, for an out-of-town wedding we had been invited to and I had forgotten to pack even a stitch of jewelry. "At least, you can wear this as a bracelet," he had said, sliding the kara off his wrist into mine.

ON THE MORNING OF APRIL 6, I dressed with care. Navy pants. Silk scarf. I even straightened my hair as if I had insider knowledge that taming my unruly curls would be the way to win over federal officials.

My husband put on a suit and a tie. He trimmed his beard and brushed his hair. This interview required both of us to be at our best.

Our destination was a tall brown building stacked with armed guards and metal detectors. An unsmiling statue of Lincoln stood across the street from it. We had clicked selfies in front of it once, many months ago.

After a short wait, we were summoned into our interview room. Together. The officer assigned to us was a white woman who looked to be in her forties. She had a pleasant and open face, a ready smile. I breathed, for what felt like for the first time in twenty-four hours.

She introduced herself and asked me several questions about my place of work. As I answered, I breathed again. I had worked at my university for years. I had even been a graduate student there. I was actively involved in campus life.

She asked to see pictures of our wedding. My husband had a set printed for exactly such a situation. He handed them to her, and she began going through them. Carefully, methodically, one picture after another, her fingers keeping steady beat.

At a close-up shot of our wedding cake, she paused. Her fingers stopped moving. I snuck in a quick glance at her face, then at the picture. Even here, inside this serious, officious building, in its flat, two-dimensional avatar, the cake looked droolworthy. Two-tiered. Chocolate ganache. Orange marmalade in one layer, salted caramel in the other. Topped with red roses and lilies. Trimmed with a red and gold ribbon.

I think I beamed a little with pride. Maybe even hunger. Did my mouth start watering? Possibly. When was the last time I had really eaten anything? Had I even had coffee that morning?

"That cake looks good," the officer said, tapping her finger lightly against the photograph.

Before I could reply, my husband said, "Thanks! It was my idea."

"*Excuse me?*" The words flew out of me before I could stop myself. He looked at me, surprised. "What?"

"What do you mean it was your idea? It most certainly wasn't."

"I am the one who suggested dark chocolate ganache."

Really? I mean, come on. Who was this guy? What was he saying? Everyone knew dark chocolate was *my* favorite. Every July, I alerted people on social media that they should stock up on it because we had entered my birthday month, and it was important that they got me worthy gifts, and what was worthier than dark chocolate? And now, here was this fellow, taking credit where none was due. He had been buying me dark chocolate for almost nine years. When we first got together, he used to say out loud to people, without the slightest bit of hesitation or embarrassment, that he loved white chocolate. As if it was a fact worth sharing. As if white chocolate was anywhere close to being real chocolate.

And how about orange marmalade? I had been in love with it since I was five years old. My parents would buy Druk's orange marmalade jam for our home in Delhi. I would slather it on toast, taking care that the ratio of marmalade pieces to bread was disproportionately high in favor of marmalade. The more the marmalade, the chewier it was inside my mouth, thus resulting in greater happiness.

I am the one who went for the cake tasting too. Where was he? In Los Angeles. Wrapping up work, sure, so he could return to Moscow and marry me. But I was the one actively living in Moscow, going to the baker—who happened to be the younger sister of one of *my* closest friends—sampling three kinds of cake, and then choosing the one I liked best. *I* had done all the work here. I had eaten my cake and made sure others got to eat it too.

I set about getting the facts straight: *Listen, you have got this all wrong. I chose our cake. Left to you, you would have chosen something offensive, like white chocolate and strawberry.*

How long did we go back and forth? A minute. Maybe five? We stopped when the officer cleared her throat loudly and waved her hand. That shut us up immediately. Clearly, she had more questions for us.

"You can go," the officer said. Was that exasperation in her voice? A tinge of I-don't-make-enough-to-sit-through-this-nonsense? "Your green card will arrive in the mail," she said. She rose, shook our hands, and nodded at the door.

Stunned, we gathered up our papers, our photos, and walked to the nearest taco stand. We took pictures of each other and our food. We stuffed our faces with carnitas and drank too much beer. We texted the good news and the pictures to my family.

Before leaving for Moscow, we stopped at The Scoop, Spokane's best-known ice cream shop. Neither of us remembers what flavors we opted for that day. But surely as I unwrapped my scarf from around my neck to avoid spilling ice cream on it, I thanked the universe for creating both chocolate and marmalade, unaware that for years to come, my husband would continue to insist that it was his choice of cake that saved our interview and our marriage. The nerve.

A TALE OF
TWO CHUTNEYS

I COME FROM WOMEN whose skills in the "womanly arts" of knitting and needlework may best be described as "modest." Neither of my grandmothers spent those long, humid afternoons in Kolkata embroidering flowers or birds. Nor did they while away autumn evenings knitting sweaters for loved ones. My mother knows how to sew buttons and mend small tears. In the early days of their marriage, she knit a sweater—maroon all over, with a white pattern near the shoulders—for my father. I am significantly less talented than that. I have knitted two scarves because I know that one basic stitch, and on a couple of different occasions I have bought embroidery kits for fun.

But where the women of my family are not known for these arts, they *are* known for their skills in the kitchen. My two grandmothers shared little in common with each other, except for the stellar tamarind pickles they made every summer (one plucked out the seeds during the process, the other kept them) and the multiple dishes they put together for every meal, a trait my mother learned and, luckily for me, inherited.

Of course, when I was growing up in the New Delhi of the 1980s and '90s, I didn't recognize the exquisite privilege inherent in this. Lunch on weekdays constituted a daal, a vegetable side dish—sometimes two, if one had been fried and served along with the daal—and a fish curry. We ate everything with rice. Sometimes for dinner, and depending on the menu, Ma replaced the rice with whole-wheat rotis.

On weekends, it was still the beautiful trinity of daal, vegetables, and a dead animal, but with ingredients that required a little more time, a tad more attention. In place of fish, we ate chicken or mutton. On rare and special occasions, it was pork.

What tipped the scale even more on weekends was when Ma made her tomato chutney. Redder than tomato soup, it was the last thing ladled onto the plate, after you had finished eating the meat. It was sweet and tangy, sharp and spicy. It cleaned your palate while also serving the glad tidings of a dessert. In other words, it was perfection.

THE WORD "CHUTNEY" comes from the Hindi word *chaat na*, meaning "to lick," and in India there are as many kinds of chutneys as there are actual people. A chutney is not a pickle. Nor is it a jam or a jelly. It may be made of mint or green chilies, coconut or peanut, date and tamarind, even onion, depending on the part of India and what's been traditionally available there.

My family comes from Bengal, where chutneys may be made from green mangoes, hog plums, pineapple, raw papaya, and my personal favorite, the humble tomato. A well-made tomato chutney is a study in contrasts. For every bite of sweetness it offers, it also sneaks in a carefully calibrated alchemy of tanginess and heat.

Family lore has it that I fell for the tomato chutney hard and fast when I was a toddler. Once at a relative's home, where we had gathered to attend a religious ceremony, I wandered into the worship room. The altar had been decked up for the gods with flowers, incense, and an elaborate spread of delicious offerings including a massive bowl of chutney. I am told I lunged for it, no doubt puzzled why such a divine food had been left unattended when all this while I could have been noshing on it.

THE FIRST TIME I truly had to figure out how to feed myself was at age twenty-three, when I moved out of my parents' home and began living on my own. My new hometown was Chandigarh, a well-planned, modern city; the capital of the twin states of Punjab and Haryana; and about five and a half hour's drive from my parents' home in Delhi. I worked as a marketing communications specialist for a gigantic multinational company. They had offices all over the world, with their Chandigarh office serving as their India headquarters.

I leased a one-bedroom apartment from a kind elderly couple. They lived on the ground floor of a two-story house and rented out the two apartments on top. I occupied the smaller one, and next to me lived a young couple with their three-year-old son.

While it did not take me long to figure out what was required of me at work, I was clueless in the kitchen. Back in Delhi, on any given day, I would wander into the kitchen multiple times to see what was being cooked and to chat with Ma. I loved food, but it had never occurred to me that I too should learn how to cook.

Nobody had put me to the task either. There was no expectation, either from my parents, or from any of my grandparents or sundry relatives, that I had to learn to cook because I was a girl. It was assumed that I would master this adult skill as and when I became an adult, just the way Baba had the first time he had moved out of Kolkata with a new job in his pocket. Ma too knew only how to boil an egg when she and Baba got married. Both my parents had picked up their culinary skills as and when they had had to. Clearly, so would I.

I wonder if my cluelessness could also be tied to a spirit of adventure I believe I inherited from my father, wherein we will eat everything at least once and we will not be picky eaters. I imagine that on the eve of leaving for Chandigarh, I assured myself there was no need to panic. I was moving from one big city to another. I could just eat like a local. It didn't occur to me that it's one thing to be adventurous when you are a traveler visiting a new city for a handful of days, and quite another when you don't have the option to leave.

MY FIRST COOKING EXPERIMENT—inside the tiny kitchen in my one-bedroom apartment in Chandigarh—involved fresh lettuce and fish. Not once in my entire life had my mother or anyone else I had known cooked these two ingredients together. But I felt brave and confident. I had watched my share of Indian, American, and British cooking shows on TV. Where was the glamour in cooking like my mother or my grandmothers? The TV chefs were all so cool, confident, and experimental. They were always cooking fish with all kinds of greens, weren't they? If they could do it, surely so could I.

I chopped up the lettuce into equal, bite-sized pieces. I simmered the fish in a pan. When it appeared to have simmered enough, I tossed in the lettuce. I let it all cook together for as long as I thought it needed.

Even now, nearly twenty years later, I feel bad for that fish. And for that lettuce. Those two poor creatures died twice: once when they were taken out of their respective natural habitats, the second time when they entered my kitchen. The goopy and puzzlingly orange dish was spectacularly underseasoned. The lettuce had turned black and bitter. So overcooked was the fish, I could have used it to prop up the books in my bedroom.

To my credit, or foolishness, I didn't let my lettuce-and-fish-curry misadventure deter me from reentering the kitchen in Chandigarh. For the nearly two years I lived there, I shopped regularly at the local market. I bought fresh fruits and vegetables. Sometimes, meat and fish too. I did always cook them even if the results were far from satisfactory. And I always, always, ate my creations. I didn't toss them in the bin, because wasting food was, and remains, the biggest crime in my book.

On rare occasions, I called Ma for directions, yet when it came to executing the steps, I resisted. I wanted to trust my own instincts. The cool chefs on TV didn't stop to ask for directions. Why couldn't

I be like them? And really, wasn't cooking supposed to be easy? Ma made it seem so. She cooked effortlessly while we chatted. We could be making fun of sundry relatives while she turned knobby potatoes into crispy fries. We could be gossiping about our neighbors, and she would transform purple eggplants into perfect golden fritters. I never saw her consult recipes. If she did, it was a quick skim of the page, and then trusting her own instincts.

Here's a thing I know now that I didn't then: it would of course have served me well to have paid even the tiniest bit of attention to Ma's actual steps and not gotten so completely lost in conversation. Not only did I not learn any cutting, chopping, or cooking techniques by osmosis; back then, I also assumed that if you *knew* good food—that is, if you ate it daily—you'd also just know how to *make* good food.

It has taken me years to figure out that, yes, while good food can indeed be simple food, you still need to know how to put that jigsaw puzzle together. You need to understand ingredients and their suitable substitutes. You need the bare-minimum right tools, pots, and pans. But mostly, you need to become a partner in that sweet marriage between patience and experience.

During my time in Chandigarh, I mostly survived on Maggi, the quick-cooking noodles beloved all over India. I would top my bowl with scrambled eggs though I longed for omelets. Not once did I manage to produce a perfect omelet. I never knew when it was time to flip the egg. Either they overcooked or they refused to budge from the pan though everything I owned was nonstick.

Night after night, my kind neighbors or my landlady tried to rescue me from my own cooking. They showed up with plates full of home-cooked meals or invited me to join them at their dinner table. Their foods were always hot and tasty, and deeply familiar to me from having grown up in Delhi. If I had come from, say, southern India, it might have taken me a while to adjust to their heavy use of wheat, dairy, and garam masala. Yet for every invitation I accepted, I graciously excused myself from several others. I didn't want them to think I was a spoiled big-city girl unable to feed herself.

IF I HAD THOUGHT that I was equipped to handle homesickness in Idaho because I had lived by myself in Chandigarh, I was proven wrong very quickly. From Chandigarh, Delhi had been less than a six-hour drive away. If I wanted to get away, I could, and I did so every other weekend. On the weekends I stayed in Chandigarh, if I didn't want to cook, all I had to do was step out of my apartment and cross the street. Within minutes, I would be engulfed in the warm embrace of one excellent restaurant after another, filled with flavors I cherished, and that anchored me to who I was and where I belonged.

In Moscow, the nearest Indian restaurants were two and a half hours away in Spokane, Washington—and terrible, at that. The only way I and my roommate—who also happened to be from India—could have Indian food was either to make it at our home or be invited over for a meal by any of the other students from India. Or to attend the annual India Night celebration on campus. Hosted by the Indian Students Association, it was an evening of songs, dances, and food that was tasty, bite-sized, and never quite enough.

ONE NIGHT a friend of a friend invited me to dinner. When I arrived at her house, I discovered to my horror that my host—a white woman in her thirties—had cooked what she insisted on calling Indian food. There were three items in all, and in each, the spices sat bitter and wrong against my palate. They had been tossed willynilly into the pan. No thought had gone into their order or quantity. Clearly, the cook had no knowledge that some spices needed to be toasted dry, others in hot oil, to release their full flavor.

It took all kinds of self-control to not cry tears of rage or frustration at the wastage, at her entitled behavior. To not say, "How dare you." The entire evening she looked pleased with herself, and at one point she leaned in to ask, "Tell me now, do I not remind you of your mother?"

That night I lay in bed, unable to fall asleep. How often had my brother and I returned home from school or college with a friend or two in tow, and Ma had cheerfully put together meals for all of us. Meals that were healthy and tasty and came together quickly. As much as she enjoyed cooking and feeding people, there was also a practical, matter-of-fact side to her when it came to food. She didn't romanticize it. She didn't mourn the absence of recipes that were gone from our lives with the passing of her mother. Ma had interests outside of the kitchen, such as the morning tea she preferred to take by herself while watching the sunrise from her balcony, or how she retreated in the afternoon to read the day's newspapers, and stepped out every evening for a walk. The well-being of her family was her priority, but so was the quiet time she spent with herself.

ONE PARTICULARLY homesick Sunday afternoon in Moscow, I called Ma to ask for her tomato chutney recipe.

She laughed and said, "That's easy."

As Ma shared the recipe, I could see what she meant. It really was not that difficult. The tomatoes needed to be cooked in a bit of mustard oil tempered with salt, sugar, and the spice mix known as paanch phoron.

When we hung up, I felt confident. I felt I could do it.

PAANCH PHORON literally means "five spices." It's a dry spice blend that tempers everything from daals to vegetables to sweetly complex chutneys. Paanch phoron can be found all through the eastern states of India, each slightly different from the next. The Bengali paanch phoron I grew up with usually comprises seeds of fennel, fenugreek, nigella, mustard, and sometimes cumin.

You may pull down the best paanch phoron from your pantry and the juiciest tomatoes from the nearest farmer's market, but they still won't make the best chutney if you don't have mustard oil—pungent at room temperature, spiky when it hits a hot pan. Without its anchoring quality, your tomato chutney will just not sing.

There is also no single way of making this chutney. While Ma's was more than adequate to make our weekends special, the same chutney when dressed up and served at Bengali weddings turned the meal decadent. This version came studded with dates, raisins, cashews, and a sweet mango leather called aam shotto. Sure, aam shotto is delicious enough that you can eat it straight out of the package. However, if you take the additional step of cutting it up into little squares and adding it to the chutney as it cooks, the heat will soften the squares and they will take on a silken, melt-in-your-mouth caramelized texture.

UNSURPRISINGLY, my first attempt at making Ma's tomato chutney ended in spectacular failure. The tomatoes didn't cook down all the way. The color didn't turn the rich dark red it needed to. Oh, and of course I didn't have either mustard oil or paanch phoron. Where was I going to get these ingredients in Moscow, Idaho? I made do with what I had. Canned tomatoes, canola oil, and whole spices that I tossed together. I partially blame Ma too. Her recipe didn't come with specific measurements. Everything was a guesstimate.

Instead of evoking that warm fuzzy feeling I had hoped it would, my chutney made me angry. And frustrated. The problem was that I had expected my mother's level of polish and sophistication from my own amateur attempt. I was too young and stupid to realize that the right ingredients and measurements mattered. That cooking was both an art as well as a science, and that just like in every other field, here too your instincts served you well, *provided* you had put in the initial work and developed them in the first place.

Over time, multiple accidents like my bland tomato chutney turned me off from trying to cook the flavors of my childhood. There simply was no point in replicating the dishes cooked by Ma or my grandmothers, was there? They were never going to taste as good. They were only going to make me feel worse and remind me of everything and everyone that was far away.

So I dove into pastas, sandwiches, and stews, and into Indian recipes that I hadn't eaten much of as a kid. It wasn't a rejection of Indian food per se or of the hospitality I had seen at my home. In imitation of my mother and my grandmothers, I hosted friends. I invited students for end-of-semester celebrations. I invited colleagues to potlucks. I fed them Moroccan chicken or beef curry. Not the summer-special daal my maternal grandmother cooked in Kolkata, or the chili chicken my paternal grandmother made on special occasions.

It seemed to work out fine. I earned some praise for my cooking. I learned new dishes. But what I didn't realize was that in denying the flavors of my childhood to my guests, I was also denying something fundamental to myself.

I CAN'T PINPOINT the moment when it all started to change.

Was it that summer of 2017 when I taught in Italy? When after a month of eating cured meats, pizzas, olives, cheeses, and pastas—as scrumptious as they were—I thought I would lose my mind if I didn't eat foods with heat and spice? So much so that the weekend my students and I went up to Florence, and I found out that I had unknowingly booked myself into a hotel across from a renowned Szechuan restaurant, I explored that gorgeous city to my heart's content, but ate all my lunches and dinners doused in that telltale chili oil.

Or was it when I moved to North Carolina from Idaho? My new hometown came with reasonably good Indian restaurants as well as international stores. If I was willing to travel to the Triangle (Raleigh, Durham, and Chapel Hill), two hours away, the number and quality of restaurants and stores shot up in the most pleasant way.

Or was it during the pandemic? When, by month 2 of lockdown, my husband and I had worked our way through all possible breakfast items to make with eggs, toast, and oatmeal, and I began watching Indian food channels on YouTube for inspiration?

All these moments led to last fall, when during my Sunday meal-preps I began making foods I grew up with in New Delhi to take for lunch in my office in North Carolina. If the first half of the week was dedicated to cauliflowers cooked with potatoes and green peas, the second half belonged to green beans sauteed with nigella seeds. When I heated these, versus, say, leftover pasta, in my office microwave, and dove in for the first bite, the difference was electrifying. It felt like I was not just nourishing my body after having lectured for three hours straight or having met with seven students one after another to go over their upcoming assignments. I was nourishing something else, something far more primal, that was alive and hungry inside my brain.

I have also had to admit to myself that for the longest time, my approach to cooking contained not just a kernel but a whole corncob of impatience. I wanted to be done in the kitchen quickly, efficiently, so I could tend to things that were "important," such as writing and reading, or tasks that paid my bills. From that first time I simmered fish and lettuce in Chandigarh, it's been a long journey to realize that there really is nothing more important than nurturing that primal, animal brain.

LAST WEEK, ten years since my first attempt, I tried my hand at making a Bengali-style tomato chutney again. My kitchen now stocks mustard oil and paanch phoron, thanks to the international store barely a mile away. Plus, I have a secret weapon: a trustworthy YouTube channel run by experts of Bengali cuisine. I play, pause, and rewatch their videos as many times as I need, and I note down exact measurements before making any purchase.

I begin by heating up my trusty nonstick wok. I pour in mustard oil, and when it ripples, I toss in one whole dried red chili, and paanch phoron. When they start sputtering, I add tomatoes. I stir as they cook and reduce. I put in a pinch of citric acid. Then, sugar, and all the other accoutrements I have gathered—cashews, raisins, dates, miraculously, even half a packet of aam shotto. When the chutney cooks through, I remove it from the heat. I cover it with a lid and let it cool.

Next, I put together my lunch plate. Rice, leftover chicken curry, and sauteed green beans. I ladle the chutney on the side. I go in for seconds. Then, thirds.

THE BOYS OF NEW DELHI

An Essay in Four Hurts

BECAUSE I WAS TWELVE

Because no one else "saw" me. Or at least that's how I felt in my neighborhood and the girls-only Catholic school I attended. I felt too big in my skin, my legs concrete pillars and not the statuesque, never-ending sexiness of the girls I envied, though I couldn't bring myself to admit it. I didn't want to be those girls. Not really. Sure, I envied their tiny waists and slim wrists, their long fingers and shapely necks. But wasn't I smarter than most of them put together?

And yet, and yet.

That summer, and in that merciless New Delhi heat, your music store was one with air-conditioning. Unlike the rival shop that was located a stone's throw away, had a larger stock of music, more space, and, overall, cuter salesmen, but zero air-conditioning. I am embarrassed to admit that your store's pleasant interiors are what drew me in the first time and not any quest for great music.

My first purchase was that Grammy Awards cassette. I wanted to pay you, remember? When I pulled out the forty-rupee note from my jeans, you chuckled. You grasped the money and shook your head. Then with a quick trick of your hand, you slid it right back. That brush of your fingers lived in my jeans for days. You smelled of cigarettes and other grown-up things that I knew my dad would disapprove of.

But I approved. You had broad shoulders and an indigo shirt. Every day as I walked up to your store, I knew you watched me through the tinted screen of your door, and in full view of your coworkers. I am sure you all laughed a bit at my expense too.

How could you not? I was a twelve-year-old kid with an enormous crush on a grown twenty-seven-year-old man. Your fingertips carried experience. You had thin lips, and I wanted their pinch around mine, the graze of your teeth on my throat.

But then one day, when I showed up as usual, you were gone. Your coworker said you had returned to your hometown to get married. You were not coming back.

In hindsight, I am grateful that all those times I came to see you, we only talked about school and music; you kept your hands and lips to yourself. That night, though, I cried like an eleven-year-old girl and not the twelve-year-old woman I thought I had become.

COMPATIBILITY

Once, when I was thirteen, I asked my friend who was fifteen if he would introduce me to his friends in the neighborhood. You know, boys his age—older, smarter, and spectacularly cool. I was able to gather up my courage and make this request of him because I remember feeling pretty good about myself that day. School had been fantastic. The kind teachers had been kind, the horrid one hadn't shown up. I had even received a certificate for winning a debate. During lunch, my best friends and I had gathered as usual at our designated spot under the leafy tree we liked to claim as ours, and all through the twenty minutes, we had laughed hysterically over the stories a classmate had shared about her new boyfriend.

Apparently he insisted on showing his devotion to her by giving her new and soppy nicknames every single day. *No way,* my friends and I promised each other. *Our future boyfriends were going to be so much cooler than that.*

After I had returned home from school, I had inaugurated a new black sweater and a purple polka-dot skirt. My hair was tousled but the right amount. There was that nip in the air signaling late October: New Delhi's sweet winter was just around the corner.

Spurred by all these good vibes, I had made my audacious request. I had asked my friend, "Hey, do you think you could introduce me to some of *your* friends?"

I still remember how quickly he shook his head; how abruptly he said, "I don't think so."

I should have dropped the subject. I should have guessed why he was looking away. Instead, I smoothed my skirt. I touched a black button on my sweater as if it was my lucky charm. I demanded answers. "Why not?"

My friend cleared his throat. He continued to look away. Finally, when he spoke, his voice was so low I had to lean my head toward him. "I am not sure," he said. "I am not sure you will be *compatible* with any of them."

This time I nodded. I dropped the subject. I knew what he meant. "Compatibility" was a big word. I was a big girl. Most days, I was ashamed of my body but confident in other aspects of myself, like my sense of humor, my ability to write well, the solid loyalty I offered my friends. But in that moment, all my qualities went away. He *was* older, smarter, more knowledgeable. What did I know of his friends, of boys who were almost young men, and who or what they found "compatible"?

Today I am a university professor. I put on a suit of confidence every day, although some days it struggles to sit properly. Semester after semester, I read essays where students write about all the ways they feel ugly in their skin. Because of that time their moms said something, or maybe it was a friend or neighbor. Or that time an influencer hyped up a product on social media and went on and on about how it helped her achieve her dream body. Or when their father pushed them to go to the gym because the only blueprint he could accept for healthy was skinny.

Oftentimes, I can't read these essays in one go. I have to take breaks. I have to steel myself. The words carry so much hurt, though they are recollecting moments from five, ten, fifteen years ago. I have a hard time associating the harsh descriptions my students use for themselves with how I see them in the classroom: confident, stylish, smart. Ready and able to take over the world. They remind me that underneath our suits, we are all a little beastly, and still deeply hurt.

That friend and I are in touch via the occasional email. He is onto his third marriage now. None of the previous marriages have lasted for more than one year, at best two. I wonder if he still closes conversations with words like "compatibility."

WINTER COAT

When I was fifteen, I bought a sweater that was red, black, and long. It went past my knees and had shiny black buttons the size of poker chips. I bought it with my allowance while wandering through the neighborhood market one evening. In the New Delhi of the 1990s, those markets with their clutch of permanent shops and a revolving array of seasonal vendors were the equivalent of the now ubiquitous mall.

It was the start of the winter season, and the red and black sweater was hanging from a plastic rope. The vendor selling it had heaped his wares on three rectangular tables. One carried colorful scarves and socks; another held hats of all shapes and sizes; the third, bright new sweaters. My eyes went straight to the red and black sweater and stayed there. Those two colors were, and still are, my favorites. I mean, has there ever been a more badass combination than red and black?

So I bought the sweater. Impulsively. Without once bargaining with the vendor.

It was a sweater but felt like a coat, the kind that men and women wore in American films, the kind you didn't find easily in New Delhi. The 100 rupees felt like a splurge, but the sweater made me feel stylish, like I was on the runway even though the world had told me repeatedly that there wasn't anything stylish about my height or girth or face.

A Man in My Life noticed my new sweater. Instead of a smile, his eyes narrowed in displeasure. He nodded curtly. Which only meant one thing. Disapproval-disappointment-waste-of-time-and-money.

So I smiled. A lot. And I talked. A lot. I chattered with Energy and Enthusiasm, the two weapons nervous people use the world over when desperate to win approval. To no avail.

The Man in My Life shook his head. He said I shouldn't wear it because it made me look fatter than I was already. He said I should return it and buy something else, maybe a scarf or a pair of socks. He even offered to come with me and help me choose.

I refused. Sure, his words wounded, but not enough to make me give up my sweater. I couldn't help it. That combination of red and black did make me feel like a stylish badass.

So The Man in My Life took to reminding me every time we went for walks. Even on days when I had done tremendous things at school, when I felt tall and regal, he said things like, "Don't wear it. It makes you look fatter. It accentuates your shortness."

These days, when I try on clothes at stores and something doesn't fit, his words settle on me like a second skin. Some days I am lucky. My plucky fifteen-year-old-self sneaks out and peels away his displeasure. Other days, she hides. His words sting until I leave the dressing room and return home empty-handed.

KIMBHUTKIMAKAR

When I was seventeen, the boy I dated told me he couldn't believe he was with someone of my shape. He called me "Kimbhutkimakar." The word doesn't mean anything, neither in English nor in Bengali, our mother tongue, but it exists. It's the name of a monster from *Abol Tabol*, a book of nonsense rhymes penned by Sukumar Ray. The original intent behind the poems, and their accompanying illustrations, was to entertain children, not hurt teenage girls with brittle confidence.

When I was a kid, my mother used to read to me those very same nonsense rhymes. I loved them so much I could recite several of them from memory. "Kimbhutkimakar" too had once been among my favorites. And why not? He had the head of a tusked elephant, a wild bushy mane, a long alligator-like tail, the hind legs of a giant bird, and his back and shoulders were covered in feathers. The poem's first line read, "This disgusting creature . . ."

Years later, face-to-face with the exaggerated paintings and sculptures of Fernando Botero, I remembered those words again. It was September of 2022, and I was in Bogota, Colombia, attending a travel writers' conference. One afternoon, while touring the city's famous La Candelaria neighborhood, I found myself at the Botero Museum, so named because most of its collection comprises works either created or collected by Fernando Botero. I stared at his "fat" Mona Lisa, easily one of his most famous paintings. He had painted her in 1978, when he was about forty-five years old. I stared at Mona Lisa's full face, thinly arched eyebrows, her eyes with their frank gaze, the tight nose, and pursed lips. I wondered how many people in Botero's youth must have pressed upon him to present human bodies in the way they have most often been celebrated in art, be it Michelangelo's uber athletic *David* or the curvaceous ivory that is Boticelli's *Venus*, and yet, for reasons best known to him, Botero painted his Mona Lisa unapologetically large.

Now, nearly twenty years later, that boy who once called me Kimbhutkimakar is the father to a little girl. I am friends with him on Facebook, where he routinely posts pictures of his wife and daughter, who link their arms with his and smile straight into the camera. Here's a picture of them eating out. There, they have gone to the movies. Yesterday they played badminton. Last month they vacationed in Paris.

I have never met either his wife or their daughter. But I wonder what names he calls them now, what words they don't repeat when they look into the camera, what echoes they will hear all their lives.

KILLER DINNER

EARLY IN THE SPRING OF 2006, while working as an editor in a publishing house in New Delhi, I received a much-awaited email: my application to the creative writing program at the University of Idaho had been accepted. All I had to do was quit my job; bid adieu to my friends, family, and entire life in India; and head to Idaho.

I got to work immediately.

I approached seven different banks for education loans, because when you convert rupees into dollars, everything is very, very expensive. But back in 2006, no Indian bank had even heard of anything called "creative writing," so all seven of my requests got rejected. By way of encouragement, one manager said to my chest, "Why don't you stop by again next week? I am sure you and I can work something out."

In the end, I gathered whatever I had saved in my four years of working as an editor—which after converting into dollars turned out to be enough for only one semester in America. All through the multiple plane rides, I thought of the many assurances I had had to give my parents: *yes, I will take good care of myself; yes, I will come back home when I run out of money; no, I will not try anything remotely risky,* but also *I absolutely must do this.*

Soon after my arrival in Moscow, Idaho, I received my first-ever dinner invitation. Granted, it wasn't exclusively for me. I was to be one of seventy or so guests—students and faculty from the creative writing department—who would gather at the home of Professors K and B, our hosts and also faculty in my department. This was their annual start-of-the-school-year potluck.

I heard from seniors in the program that this was *the* social event of the year. There would be excellent food, wine, and revelry, plus several rounds of something called leg-wrestling. Apparently Professor K, besides being the recipient of several writing honors, was an undefeated leg-wrestling champion. It didn't matter whether you were male or female, young or old, whether your legs resembled toothpicks or Athenian columns. Your leg was not going to win against Professor K's.

I accepted the invitation, mostly because no matter how hard I tried, I couldn't picture any of my own erstwhile professors, clad in saris or salwar-kameez, getting down on the floor and leg-wrestling with students of any gender, especially in front of an audience, and then permitting said audience to tell other people about it for years to come.

On the appointed day, Polly—a new friend and second-year fiction writer—picked me up. She had baked a peach cobbler, and all through the drive it sat on my lap, swaddled like a baby in blue-and-white-striped towels. I had never eaten a peach cobbler. (Had I ever eaten a peach? I couldn't remember.) I couldn't conjure the shape or appearance of the cobbler under the towel. The only cobbler I had known in New Delhi sat inside a makeshift shop by our neighborhood gate and mended broken bags and sandals. I couldn't imagine what forces had brought together a fruit and him, or someone like him, to create something with this heady, cinnamon-thick scent. For the entire fifteen or so minutes of our drive, I breathed it in, recognizing the telltale signs of a lifelong romance.

Professors K and B's home sat atop Palouse Range, located north of our picturesque university town. It was a beautiful drive, like others I'd enjoyed so far in Idaho, and Polly expertly maneuvered her car through tree-lined, winding paths. Palouse Range was a few degrees colder than Moscow proper, and I shivered, not only because my tropical body hadn't yet acclimatized to these temperatures but also because I had heard that bears and moose were frequent visitors in this area.

With warm hugs, Professor K welcomed us inside her home. Professor B waved from the deck. Professors in India don't hug, at least mine didn't, and you never addressed them by their first names. *Baby steps*, I steadied myself, *baby steps*.

Polly and I weren't late, but the house was already packed. If this had been India, we would have easily been among the first guests to arrive, with others trickling in all through the evening. I looked around hungrily, greedily, taking in the details. This was my first-ever visit inside an American home. What if this was also my last? I had to remember this all, if not for anything else, just to be able to tell my mother everything.

Knots of guests were gathered around the colorful kitchen, in the living room, and around the dining table. A big group surrounding Professor B was smoking and drinking beer. There were stacks of books on the coffee table, and along all the walls. It was a gorgeous home, clearly adored by everyone who lived here and visited. The stunning views offered by every window—of surrounding mountains and unknown cities twinkling in the distance—took my breath away. If only I could teleport my own mother here! She would have pointed to the kitchen island and gushed, "Oh, look, just like you see in the Food Network shows."

I mingled, talking to classmates I had gotten to know, introducing myself to professors with whom I had exchanged emails from India. I tried every food I had never eaten before—lasagna, huckleberry pie, and that peach cobbler.

When it was time for leg-wrestling, I too joined the cheering crowd on the deck. It's been fifteen years since that evening, and though I can no longer remember how many people challenged

Professor K, or how long the contest lasted, this I remember: she won every single round. Hook, grip, and, finally, pull.

No bear or moose came down to check me out that evening, though the temperatures kept dropping as the hours passed. Just as I was done delivering the last of my goodbyes and we began walking over to the car, my eyes shot up to the sky. Stars jostled for space, like commuters on a New Delhi bus on a Monday morning, impatient for air, for an extra inch of space. I didn't know what the days ahead were going to bring my way, but in that moment, coming to Idaho seemed like the best decision I had ever made.

I MET STUART AND SANDRA a week after the party. Like me, they were browsing the aisles of the crowded bookstore downtown. They were in their fifties, dressed identically in faded blue jeans a few sizes too big, T-shirts, and baseball caps. They were arguing over which books to buy. When I saw Arundhati Roy's *The God of Small Things* among the ones they were considering, I offered my two cents. I had read it the year it had won the Man Booker Prize, the same year I had turned seventeen and grown very distracted by boys and thoughts of which college I would attend the following year. Sure, I had read the novel, but whether I had understood its brilliance was an entirely different matter.

That's what I told Stuart and Sandra as they paid for their books. We made our way outside the bookstore and chatted for a long time standing by the door. They were professors on my campus, though they did not have anything to do with my department. They asked specific questions about India, such as how many languages I spoke, and if I had a favorite daal recipe. In my time in Idaho thus far, I had already had to answer jaw-droppingly ignorant questions such as "Is India a country or a continent? Have you ever had ice cream? Does your family own an elephant?" Answering Stuart and Sandra's questions, founded as they were on genuine interest and knowledge, felt like monsoon showers on the parched landscape of my homesick soul.

AFTER THAT FIRST MEETING, in the manner of small towns everywhere, the three of us kept running into each other. Both husband

and wife embodied the Absent-Minded Professor trope, from the giant tear on the back of Sandra's jacket—clearly the result of an ironing accident—to Stuart's food-stained, crumbs-laden mustache and shirts. I assumed they repaired their shoes, and also cut their own hair—whenever they remembered they had to, that is. Sometimes it was hard to maintain conversation with them because they switched topics abruptly, and seemingly without meaning to, excluding anyone who wasn't them. It was as if their tongues had to constantly scramble to keep pace with their brains.

I thought Stuart and Sandra were funny, unique, and endearing. I couldn't get enough of them. My roommate, Manasi, the biologist, did not share my sentiments.

After every encounter with Stuart and Sandra, I would gush to her, "Don't you think they are brilliant? They don't waste time on stupid things like the rest of us. I wish I could be like them."

Manasi would simply nod. Sharp as a tack, she had become my best friend overnight. She had already been in the US for a year longer than I had. "You are fine as you are," she would say.

ONE DAY, when I ran into Stuart and Sandra outside my favorite coffee shop, Sandra said, "What do you think about cooking an Indian meal together?"

"Great idea," I said.

In those early days of grad school, I had neither a phone nor a computer. But kind, wonderful Manasi let me borrow her laptop every day. I used it to do my homework, to Google Chat with friends back home, and Yahoo Chat with Ma and Baba. That evening, I used her laptop to email our home address to Stuart and Sandra.

Sandra wrote back the next day. She had copied Stuart in the email. She explained in detail why she wanted us to cook Indian food in the first place: because it was "easy," she said, and because she and Stuart "cooked it all the time." Stuart chimed in too. He counted the number of friends he had personally introduced to "Indian food."

I was not sure what to do with their explanations and backstories. In our three-week-long association thus far, not once had it occurred to me to ask Stuart and Sandra—two middle-aged white professors who had never been to India—about their thoughts on what I simply called "food," and what had sustained generations of my family.

Why would I? Why was it important for me to know whether they found my food "easy" or "difficult," whether they had introduced it to one friend or fifty enemies? It would be like catching hold of the Thai woman I had met during international student orientation and telling her about my limited knowledge and experience of Thai food. As if she should care about my opinion. As if my ability to follow a Thai recipe and re-create it in my kitchen could match her innate familiarity with and ownership of it.

Another round of emails later, we decided on a date and menu. Sandra would cook mung daal; Stuart, a pot of basmati rice; and I, a turmeric-and-cumin-spiced cauliflower-potato curry. I wouldn't have to cook anything in advance. It would all happen in their kitchen. "It's huge," Sandra added reassuringly. "There is plenty of space for all of us to spread out."

As the day drew closer, my excitement rose proportionately. I imagined another bright, colorful kitchen; a living room softened with rugs and leather sofas; and windows offering gorgeous views of open skies, pine trees, and well-maintained gardens.

Mostly, I imagined the smells. Basil and truffle oil, peach cobbler, and bacon. Smells still not that familiar to me, but appetizing nevertheless. It was going to be an evening filled with stimulating conversation, great food, and wine. I couldn't wait.

ON THE APPOINTED FRIDAY, at a quarter to five, Stuart arrived to pick me up. I had only ever seen him and Sandra walk to places, since our downtown and university were eminently walkable, so I didn't know what vehicles they owned or drove.

Stuart's van was the kind I had only seen in American movies up to that point. Dark brown, it was the length of the perpetually hungry T-rex from *Jurassic Park*. It had dusty, dirty, tinted glass windows, doors that protested when forced open, and paint chipped so uniformly you'd think the resulting pattern was intentional. You could imagine such a van belonging to a middle-rank gangster, someone who had run out of favor with the boss, though early on he had shown promise.

Sandra arrived a few minutes later, damp hair pasted to her red, fiercely panting face. She'd ridden her bike up the hilly road that connected her office on campus to my apartment. When she pulled off her helmet and jacket, sweat ran down her prominent forehead, large nose, and chin. I invited her inside my apartment so she could join Stuart, who now sat at my dining table, rifling through an old *National Geographic*.

Sandra refused. She waited at the door, dripping on the mat. Stuart waved at his wife. She waved back, and he returned to the magazine while I gathered my keys, my purse, and the canvas bag I had packed with the spices, potatoes, and cauliflower.

"Hurry up, please," Sandra said, tapping her feet to an urgent, erratic rhythm. "We will be late for dinner."

On hindsight, that should have been my first clue. I should have realized that anyone who can rush you at quarter to five, on a Friday evening, does not have a fun, relaxed dinner in mind. That we would not be cooking like they did on American movies and TV shows, where happy, friendly people, full of smiles, cooked while drinking wine from oversized goblets, and every now and then threw their heads back and laughed out loud while popping tiny, delicious appetizers into their mouths.

I should have also known, instinctively, that this wouldn't be the kind of dinner party my parents threw either—where the entire multicourse menu was ready by afternoon, thereby freeing the hosts to hang out with the guests, and foods were warmed up and served as the evening progressed.

Already, in this one month in the US, I had been both amused and horrified by some of the food habits I had witnessed, such as adults drinking milk at mealtimes, or ice cream portions the size of basketballs. But the hardest one for my urban Indian soul, used to eating dinner late, was this American business of eating dinner at five. Especially on Fridays. I mean, even nine-year-old me was cooler than this.

"Look, Sandra," I wanted to snap. "It's August. It's 5 p.m. Do you see how bright and sunny it is outside? It's criminal to eat dinner at this hour. Plus, what kind of host scolds her guest before she has even had a chance to do something truly disappointing?"

Of course, I didn't say any of that. Reprimand a host, especially a professor? Never. What would my well-mannered, cultured, good Indian parents say?

Here's what I should have done, though: I should have lied.

I should have told a white lie, something small and uncomplicated, the kind of detail that earnest foreigners might believe about Indians, provided you delivered it with sincerity and unbroken eye contact. Something like "I am so sorry, but my religion does not permit me to eat at other people's homes on ___ days. Please, may we reschedule?"

Given Stuart and Sandra's interest and knowledge of India, it's possible that I would have had to improvise and throw in a couple of additional, believable details while also making sure I didn't come across as trying too hard.

I locked my apartment. I told myself to get over Sandra's tone. Maybe she had had a rough day. What did I know? Maybe their son was home, possibly getting hangrier by the minute. He didn't grow up in New Delhi. He couldn't have known that only children and boring people ate dinner before nine o'clock. For him, this *was* dinnertime. I had never met him, but I had vivid memories of when my younger brother was fourteen. If no one else was home and he brought along his friends, the onus of helping those smelly, stinky boys figure out snacks fell on me, especially if they were exhausted from playing soccer or some such nonsense. Like I tried to explain to my mother once, it was a testament to how much I liked those kids and respected their choices—and not a reflection of my own laziness—that I let them haphazardly ransack her well-organized, just recently stocked-up fridge, to figure out what to feed themselves.

OUT IN THE PARKING LOT, Sandra unlocked her bike. Stuart climbed into the van and clicked open the passenger door. I glanced at Sandra and waited. Surely she was going to slide her bike somewhere in the back or clip it to the rooftop. This much I had learned in my time so far: Americans were geniuses when it came to carrying their vehicles. I was still in awe of how many bikes the city buses carried on their front racks, like mechanical mama giraffes, perfectly suited to our vehicle-obsessed times.

Stuart started the van. Sandra waved her hand to indicate I should sit next to him. I hopped in. Sandra shut my door, making no move to enter the van herself. I knocked on the glass separating us. She flapped her hand, urging us to go.

Confused, I turned to Stuart. "Do you need to unlock the back door? Sandra is still outside."

Stuart shook his head. "Oh, she won't enter the van."

"Why not?" I grabbed the seatbelt, as he started pulling out of the parking lot. The buckle didn't latch, so I held it across my torso like a pageant winner's sash. Miss Most Recent Arrival. Miss Fresh off the Boat. Miss About to Eat Dinner at Five.

I rolled down the window and called out, "Sandra, aren't you coming?"

"No," Sandra said, hopping onto her bike. "I'll see you at home. No van ride for me. I don't wish to contribute to global warming."

But the van is going to your home, and whether it transports two people or three, its contribution to global warming will remain the same. The polar bears will live, Sandra. The tsetse flies will mate again too.

Of course, this too I swallowed. Americans, I had learned, were prickly about personal space and being told to do things. It was best to drop the issue.

ONCE WE HIT THE MAIN ROAD, I looked around surreptitiously. The inside of the van smelled of dust, unwashed clothes, old socks, and some kind of animal, though I couldn't be sure. Growing up, whenever my brother and I broached the subject of a pet, our mother always said, "You two are animal enough for me." I had read that Americans kept unusual pets, like pythons and tigers, so I held my breath and braced myself for whatever was coming next.

At the first traffic light, I caught sight of Sandra in my rearview mirror, no more than a speck, but I could tell it was her, a tight pinprick of helmet, jacket, and handlebars against a backdrop of vast sunshine.

In a few minutes, Stuart turned right. The street narrowed, and beautiful homes sprung up on both sides. The van slowed considerably, and I tried to guess which house was theirs. This was my first time in this neighborhood, but it looked like others I had walked through, the kind of tidy American neighborhoods one saw on TV. Neat rows of two-story houses; multicolored garbage bins on wheels; the peculiar pull-out mailboxes, lawns with trimmed flowerbeds, swing sets, toys, and BBQ grills; and one to two cars in the driveway.

Stuart pulled into a skinny driveway and turned off the engine.

"Thank you," I said, and meant it. No more sitting inside the car, smelling whatever I had been smelling. I returned my sash-seatbelt to its corner, grabbed my purse and the food bag, unlocked my door, and stepped out.

The garden/lawn, choked with weeds and overgrown grass, had probably not been mowed in years. A sad, forlorn light glowed from somewhere inside the house, as if the residents had invested in the tiniest, most unimpressive bulb they could find. It had the lowest wattage of all the options in the market, but after purchasing and installing it, they had found even that to be too much, and had wrapped it in rags they had previously used to clean their oven.

The house itself was straight out of the cover of my copy of Nathaniel Hawthorne's *House of Seven Gables*. I could see it sitting on my bookshelf back home, the picture as clear today in my mind's eye as back then: the colors, black and indigo; the house, tall and imposing under a moody, dark sky; a window on the top floor aglow from a pale golden light; a woman in an old-fashioned dress holding a lantern in her left hand and facing the house as if taking its measure; in the foreground, a rat looking up at the woman; a gargoyle looking down at the rat; and, swirling through it all, broad swatches of mist.

A light went on in my brain. This haunted house was not really Stuart and Sandra's. This was owned by the university, and I was the subject of a good old-fashioned prank. These two professors had been assisted in this endeavor by my department, as well as our campus. They did this every year; pulled pranks on new, unsuspecting students, broadcast it via hidden cameras on local channels, and had a good laugh. I just happened to be this year's candidate. This wasn't personal. This was silly, playful, and totally harmless.

Another thought occurred to me. As important as it was for these Americans to have fun at my expense, it was doubly important for me to uphold India's honor.

"Bring it," I said to the house. I would enter this minefield with a smile, and no matter what happened inside, I would not lose my composure. I would not display any anxiety or panic. Otherwise these Americans would surely target more Indian students to prank next year. No, I couldn't let that happen. I wouldn't. Pranks like these were water on my duck-like back. Here now, gone in a second.

"DO YOU NEED HELP?" Stuart asked, grabbing his weather-beaten briefcase from the back seat.

"Oh no," I said, perhaps a little too cheerfully. "I have everything I need right here." I raised my bag like a flag.

I followed Stuart into the darkened house. It took my eyes a while to adjust, but once they did, and because Stuart turned on more lights, all illusions (and hopes) of pranks and reality shows vanished. This *was* their actual home. There was evidence everywhere— art and photographs on walls, old birthday decorations, a map of Asia at the end of World War II, backpacks and grocery bags, and laundry—piles and piles of it, on the loveseat, on the floor, bundled like a retired yeti next to the TV, spilling out of baskets, washed or unwashed, who could tell? This much was clear: the people who lived in this house were the same people who drove that van.

Stuart gestured expansively. "We straightened up because you were coming. Sandra should be here shortly."

Like magic, Sandra appeared. She took off her helmet and jacket and clapped her hands like a drill sergeant. "Conrad," she shouted, "come and say hello! We have company."

I had not realized that there was anyone in the room besides the three of us. But now their son Conrad emerged, slowly, from behind the loveseat, an anaconda unspooling itself to come to its full height, albeit with a magazine in his hands. He had on tomato-red velvet pants, a forest-green full-sleeved shirt buttoned at the wrists, and a beanie that didn't quite cover his thin, long hair.

If you ever drive out of New Delhi toward the fields of neighboring Punjab, you will see tall, skinny scarecrows with giant earthen pots for heads. Often lopsided, they are not the best ambassadors of India's architectural and or engineering marvels. Which is why I doubt they scare anyone or anything, let alone the notorious crows and pigeons of northern India. Perhaps, at this point, the birds have reached that stage of their evolutionary process where they have elected to let us live with our delusions. They see the scarecrows as quality entertainment. Or as props when they have to train their fledglings.

Conrad was one such scarecrow.

I extended my right hand. "Hi, Conrad, nice to meet you," I said.

Conrad stared somewhere between my left ear and shoulder. When he shook my hand, his inch-long fingernails grazed my skin.

"Were you reading?" Stuart asked with a big grin.

Conrad looked miserable in our company, as if it was the most natural thing in the world to read in the dark, pressed between the wall and loveseat.

"Well, carry on," Stuart said, cheerfully, "We'll be cooking for a while."

Conrad returned to his spot without collapsing the laundry pile closest to him, piled high with his mother's worn-out bras and underwear.

This time both Stuart and Sandra led the way. I tightened my grip on my bag and followed.

SANDRA HADN'T LIED. Theirs was indeed a large kitchen, suffused with plenty of natural light, two refrigerators, and enough counter space for a joyous, invigorating, full-blown party. Ah, what my college friends and I could have done with such a place.

She waved her hand and explained the two refrigerators. "One is for the organic produce we buy every Saturday. The other is for milk and eggs, that kind of stuff." She opened the fridges to show me, as if I was about to challenge her claim and she needed to set me right.

The one containing dairy items looked like everyone else's fridge.

There were milk jugs, yogurt and cottage cheese, and a small block of butter.

The stench hit as soon as Sandra opened the second fridge. I could make out the contours of leaves and stems here and there, but overall, the contents had turned black a long time ago. Yes, once upon a time the fruits and vegetables may have been green and other colors, but now they reminded me of naturally occurring black things, like bears, coal, and hair.

"Where shall we begin?" Sandra asked, rummaging inside the fridge I still see in my nightmares.

This time the lie came quickly. "It would be inappropriate for me to take back the cauliflower and potatoes I have brought with me," I said. "They are meant for tonight's dinner. Not using them would be dishonorable."

It worked.

Sandra closed the fridge. She brought out a plastic container and poured out a cup of uncooked daal. Across from me, Stuart began preparing the rice.

Just then, a horde of cats entered the kitchen. Two jumped up on the countertops; a third began rubbing itself against my legs.

I froze.

With the same hands with which they had been handling food, Stuart and Sandra now started tending to their cats. They petted them all over, cooed into their necks, offered treats, and let their feline babies lick their human fingers. I thought of the images of India most prevalent in the West, how uncleanliness is often such a dominant theme. Yet what was I witnessing here? Two well-educated college professors prepping food for themselves and their guest while their hands were slick with cat saliva.

Here's a fact Stuart and Sandra didn't know about me: I am terrified of cats. It's not their fault they didn't know. The subject just never came up. The New Delhi neighborhoods in which I grew up, no more than two or three families had pets. So inquiring about pets wasn't programmed into my system.

Don't ask why. I won't be able to tell you why I hate cats, why it is that I imagine them ganging up against me and chewing through my bone and muscle until reaching my lungs and other internal organs and enjoying them for breakfast, lunch, and dinner. I didn't suffer any cat-induced traumatic incident in childhood, at least not one that either my parents or I remember. The only explanation I can offer is that my mother hates and fears them too. I remember her recoiling from cats in our neighborhood. It didn't matter whether they were stray or belonged to someone. In her daily life, Ma wasn't the least bit superstitious, but if a cat was nearby, she gave it a wide berth, especially at night. If we happened to be out for a walk and a cat appeared, glowing eyes and all, Ma would freeze or duck behind my father. To this day, she too doesn't know why she feels this way. Who is this long-gone ancestor whose trauma Ma and I have inherited? Whose horror has our DNA adopted with eyes shut tight and arms wide open?

AT DINNER THAT NIGHT, as the cats jumped up and down Stuart's and Sandra's laps and ate off their plates, I nibbled on the curried cauliflower and potatoes. At least I knew I had practiced good hygiene. So as to not be rude, I ate a tiny bit of the rice and lentils they had cooked, trying hard to not imagine that I was ingesting cat germs with every grain.

Across from me sat Conrad. He looked at me occasionally but otherwise talked only to his parents—about school and upcoming tests—and ate using both hands and no silverware. Every now and then, he paused to examine the flecks of food that had burrowed under his nails. Then he licked his fingers, one by one, to safely transfer the contents into his mouth.

By this time, my inner monologue had boiled down to a single sentence: "Thou shalt not use whatever it is they call bathroom in this house." I didn't have to use it to know that the horrors of the house and van were going to pale in comparison. But of course, our bodies are our biggest betrayers. As soon as we were done with dinner, I needed to pee.

Sandra directed me to "the bathroom upstairs." With every step I took on the dusty, carpeted staircase, I begged for a miracle. I thought of the advice Baba had given me four years ago when I was about to enter the job market for the very first time. "Pay close attention to the state of their bathrooms and how the office treats its staff. If the bathrooms aren't tidy or the so-called unimportant people are treated poorly, walk away. No matter how much salary they offer you."

The bathroom stood directly across from Conrad's bedroom. He sat on his bed, watching, as I struggled to shut the door with its broken latch. When I propped empty shampoo bottles against the door to rig myself a barricade, he no doubt heard that too.

In that moment, I thought of that bank manager in India who had told me to keep visiting him, who had talked only to my breasts during the entirety of our conversation. I thought of the entitlement behind his gaze, how safe and powerful he must have felt in the little world where he was king.

BY THE TIME I came back downstairs, I was ready to go home, but my hosts weren't ready to release me. They had already planned their next offering. "The entertainment," Sandra called it.

I spent the next two hours sandwiched between Stuart and Sandra on their laundry-strewn loveseat. At Sandra's insistence, we watched recordings of obscure European contests, such as cheese rolling and mock gladiatorial fights. At any other point in my life, I would have had the humor and good grace to clap and cheer for the contestants, but in that moment, exhausted, homesick, and still very hungry, I felt trapped and resentful.

I thought of the two years I had put into researching creative writing programs in the United States, the sixty or so professors I had emailed to get a sense of their campuses, the tests I had taken to prove that I was indeed fluent in English, the many financial and bureaucratic hurdles I had maneuvered so I could study abroad in a post-9/11 world, the job I loved that I had quit, the loving family and friends I had left behind, the completely out-of-the-blue new job offer that had landed in my lap a week before I had left for Idaho, and the rate at which my hard-earned savings were running out of my pocket every day.

And all of that to what end? For this moment on this loveseat, squeezed and miserable between two people, like a commuter on a packed New Delhi bus on a Monday morning.

But I didn't dare leave.

For one, I wasn't sure I could find my way back home, and I didn't want to risk getting lost. But also because I was still learning the rules of being in the US, about what it meant to be a guest at someone's home here in Idaho, and not just anyone, but two professors at my university, who were no doubt acquainted with, if not friendly with, my own professors. I didn't know then how long I would last in the program and in Idaho. After all, my money was guaranteed to run out by December. What if any bad behavior on my part caused my time to be shortened even more?

I thought of how different things would have been if this was India, if Stuart and Sandra had been guests at my parents' home. How Ma and Baba would have gone out of their way to make them feel special, not only because they are that hospitable to everyone but also because, in their eyes, there's no one more important than an educator.

When I returned home that evening, Manasi was cooking dinner. I thanked her for eating late, like my family back in New Delhi. Over clean food, devoid of cat fur and cat saliva, we laughed over my misadventures at Stuart and Sandra's. In the safety of our apartment, I shrugged it off and went to sleep.

OVER THE YEARS, the saga of that evening has become a funny story to tell at parties. But in all my retellings, I have sensed that I am missing something. It's as if I myself haven't fully understood all the reasons behind my acute discomfort that night or the awkward comedy that was Stuart and Sandra's hospitality.

When Sandra had first suggested we get together to cook Indian food, I had agreed without thinking it over for a second. It had stemmed from a combination of loneliness and homesickness, and because I desperately wanted to re-create in Idaho the large group of friends I had left behind in India.

But it was also because in those initial months in the US, I considered it my duty to represent India in the best possible light. I wanted to tell every American, "Don't believe everything you see on television or read in newspapers. There is so much more to my country. There is so much more to me. Don't buy into the stereotypes, please. Give me a chance. No, don't give me your pity. Give me your time. I will share with you my food, culture, festivals. Hand in hand, with you, for you, I will take my first steps toward becoming a model minority."

FIFTEEN NOTES
ON A DAY JOB

1

WHEN I WAS EIGHTEEN, the most boring professor in the world taught me American history. She was a scholar, yes, laden with more degrees than the earth has tectonic plates, but an inspiring teacher, that she was not. At the designated hour each day, she would enter our classroom, sheathed in yet another handwoven sari, in colors as vibrant as fire and cinnamon. She would glance around the room giving us all the benefit of her gaze, and I suspect, the time to admire her exquisite taste in wardrobe and hand-forged silver jewelry. She would set down her purse, seat herself behind the desk, and take attendance. Then she would open her notebook and begin to read, slowly, so that we could not only follow along but also take notes—long, detailed notes made up of long, detailed sentences.

For fifty minutes, thrice a week, our classroom was saturated with the singsong quality of her voice, interspersed with the furious scratching from two kinds of pens: those that were afraid they would miss a word here, an important detail there, if they so much as got distracted for a second, and others, like mine, that didn't care, that only pretended, that may have even run out of ink the week before and hadn't bothered with a refill. The pens, whether well behaved or otherwise, got a reprieve only when one of the front benchers asked a question.

In the few minutes the professor took to answer, we would lean back into our chairs, stretch our fingers, and gift our hands a much-earned, much-longed-for respite. But the moment the answer wrapped up, so did our happiness. The professor would return to her notebook, drawn to it by the kind of attachment that usually inspires epic poems, and then once again she would plug up the space between our ears with the droning static of her voice.

Sitting at my usual spot, next to one or other of my closest friends, I would glance at my watch, at the clock above our professor's head, and at the pages of my own notebook, where lived the newest doodle of her face with a foghorn for a mouth. Outside the window, the pristine and inviting lawn would shimmer like a mirage, whispering words such as "just a few more minutes" and "hang in there." I would stare at that jade grass, at the blades so shiny and full of life, and vow for the millionth time that I would never ever become a college professor.

2

Ten years later, I stood before a college classroom, taking in the sight of the thirty-five American students I was going to teach that fall semester. They were all freshmen and mostly eighteen years old, except for the one gentleman who was in his sixties. In his introduction, he informed us that thirty years ago, he and his backpack had spent three months in Bangalore, India. I could tell from his tone that his three-months-fueled expertise on everything Indian was going to guide us throughout the semester and be repeated often, for the benefit of us all, but mostly me.

My students, including him, had come from all corners of the West: Idaho, Utah, Montana, Oregon, Washington, Alaska, and California. None of them had ever had a professor from India.

Unnecessarily, but perhaps understandably, I had placed double the pressure on myself in my first-ever teaching job. I was going to put my best foot forward not only for my own sake but also for the billion people I was representing. I had to be the very best I could, because if I messed up, surely my students were going to think poorly of all Indians. I couldn't allow that.

An image flashed before my eyes, a stick-figure me against a backdrop of a billion stick figures—all of them brown, fiercely opinionated, and holding up signs that said some or the other version of "Don't let us down." I wiped my sweaty, clammy hands on my red shirt. I looked at my white audience. I thought, "Shit."

3

I landed my adjunct gig soon after I earned my graduate degree in creative writing. Several people told me I was lucky. Of course, I was. To land a job, any job, in academia is the same as winning the lottery. Plus, how many people get to actually use their degrees so soon after graduation?

I was still so naive in both America and academia that I didn't really know what it meant to be an adjunct. I assumed that if I did three things correctly—taught my classes well, volunteered for various causes and initiatives for my department and the university at large, and ensured that my own creative work appeared regularly in literary journals and magazines and eventually in a book—in a few years' time I would at least be considered for promotion.

Like me, you might be unaware of an adjunct's role, so here are some specifics: an adjunct is hired on semester-long contracts. Depending on the institution, they may teach anything from two to five courses per semester. The renewal of their contract depends on a variety of factors, including the size of student enrollment and the quality of one's teaching evaluations. Generally, by hiring an adjunct, the university does not have to bother with "minor" annoyances such as paying for their health insurance.

Still, I considered myself lucky. I didn't have to commute between several sister institutions to make ends meet. I could stay put at one institution. I got to teach a wide variety of classes of my own choosing. My supervisors were friendly and approachable. A handful of my senior colleagues served as my mentors, and I went to them frequently for advice. Most others knew my name. One engaged with everything I posted on Facebook but never recognized me when we ran into each other on campus. (Really, I shouldn't say more, because that story I am saving for a novel.)

4

An aspect of adjuncting that feels unnecessarily cruel and that may be more common across universities than I want to believe is that no matter how successful the faculty member might be as a teacher and a scholar, they are not eligible for teaching awards or professional development programs, even though one might argue that they are the ones who need that guidance the most.

One year, encouraged by a friend who worked in the international programs office, I applied to teach a summer semester in Italy. My application was among several others that the institute in Italy was going to evaluate before selecting the one that best suited their overall program. A colleague—white, male, several years my senior and with one of the highest salaries on campus—admonished me, saying it was unfair of me to even apply, because I was taking away opportunities from tenure-track and tenured faculty members such as himself.

To this day, seven years later, when I work someplace else and I am no longer an adjunct, the cruelty and entitlement of that scolding stings. It serves as a reminder that kindness and empathy cannot be taught, no matter how far one may have come in life and achieved.

5

For the sixteen semesters I worked as an adjunct, I was the only professor from India for most of my students. In some cases, I was their only international professor for the entirety of their four years of college. Sometimes, in class, we compared the sizes of our hometowns and the populations within their boundaries. My students' answers ranged anywhere from 600 to 4 million people. One year, someone said, "Fifty," right after I said, "Fifteen million." We each looked at the other with something close to pity.

6

Every semester, the first day of class unfolded in a similar fashion. I read through the syllabus and taught my students how to say my name. They, in turn, introduced themselves and shared where they were from. Together we checked out the library's website. I pointed them in the direction of my office. I told them that my classroom was a no-phone zone. *If I catch you with your head down, smiling or frowning at your crotch, I will know you have your phone out.*

Typically the students laughed. They thought I was joking. A few weeks into the semester, though, when I threw the first offender out of the classroom, their laughs disappeared.

On days when students gave their presentations, I would sit in the back row, eyes fixed on their slides, my hand bent over my notebook, taking notes, jotting questions, and assigning points.

What did I really want to do, though? Pull my phone out of my pocket and scroll, scroll, scroll, through Instagram and Facebook, check what's trending on Twitter. Ignore the billion stick figures who were holding up signs that said, in big block letters, "Hypocrite."

7

Because it was the 2010s and because I hadn't grown up in this America, my students taught me all I ever needed to know about Ugg boots, man buns, and other essentials. They trained me to tell a hipster from a hippie, an emo from a goth, a nerd from a dork. The six girls with identical white shorts and beachy-wave hair talked to me about freedom. And so did the boys whose oversized pajamas said, "Beer University."

Inside the main library on campus, where I went nearly every day to read, prep for classes, and check out books, I overheard all sorts of conversations.

"Is a bibliography the same as a biography?"

"I know I am a journalism student, and I am supposed to read newspapers and stuff. But I don't, you know. I just can't."

"I need a Lion King tattoo. I don't have any money really for food, or rent, but I just need a Lion King tattoo."

"My plan was to put in the least effort and still get As. Turns out you don't get something just because you wish for it. I am mostly getting Cs."

"I really want to be a college professor. You study stuff once, and that's it. You are set for life."

8

I learned that some girls disguised their nervousness under thick layers of makeup. Their bling-bling jeans acted as shields, the hair tousled just so they could detract attention from themselves and hide from homesickness, loneliness, insomnia. In the margins of their journals, they doodled hearts and stars, reminding me of the drawings I used to make of professors with foghorn mouths once upon a time, many years ago.

Later in the semester, the same girls wrote about bad roommates, unfair bosses, alcoholic parents, and cheating partners. They mourned for high school relationships that didn't work out, all the ways in which their childhood rooms no longer felt like their own, and the specific heartbreak of coming to university and having to leave their pets behind. Often their stories kept me up at night, such as those of suicide pacts among friends, and of coaches crossing lines they shouldn't.

A few years later, some of these students would find me on places such as LinkedIn. They would send me "I would like to connect with you" messages from Seoul and Shanghai and a hundred other cities I have never been to.

Others I would see around town. Either we would wave and chat, or they would pretend not to recognize me when they asked with industrial politeness, "Paper or plastic?"

9

Most mornings, I assured myself that I did not inherit the mantle of "Most Boring Professor in the World" from my own former professor. I counted the ways in which I was different.

   i. I did not dictate notes.

  ii. I made eye contact with all my students.

 iii. I did not wear handmade saris.

 iv. I had very few pieces of hand-forged silver jewelry.

  v. I typically broke up the fifty-minute session with three activities: *Please form yourselves into groups and discuss these three questions. Let us now move on to a writing exercise. Who wants to share what they wrote? Let me show you this essay I read last night. What's the best thing you watched in the last twenty-four hours? How did it inspire you? Take your notebooks, no, not your phones, and go outside. Observe. Eavesdrop. Write.*

10

There were other mornings, too, when I would wake up with only four hours of sleep, too tired to walk to campus. I would take the bus instead, and the only way I could keep moving from one class to the next was through numerous cups of coffee.

Inside the classroom, I would be greeted by eyes glassier than mine. Students would yawn, fidget, and crane their necks to check the clock in the corner.

On those days, I *knew* I droned on, sounding exactly like my own former professor. I wish I looked half as regal as her as I rifled through notes and past lessons in my head. *Help! Someone, please, help. How do I bring these glassy eyes back to life? How do I feign my own interest?*

11

Some students wrote with such grace and intelligence they rattled my insides like a maraca, their words like seeds that shook my soul. Others made me worry about why they cared so little about the stories they carried, who they had been in the past versus who they were now, who they could be in the future, and what in particular was holding them back.

Miraculously, every time I felt disillusioned, I was gifted a moment of grace. Like that afternoon in the cafeteria when I was perusing lunch options and, unbeknownst to me, a student cashier mistook my hesitation as my inability to pay. Five or so minutes later, by which time I had almost reached my department building without having purchased any food, I turned around to find him running up the steps behind me, boxed lunch in hand. "This is for you," he said, and ran away before I could thank him.

12

Most days, I loved most of my students. Because of my own interdisciplinary background, I got to teach classes in English, history, and world studies. It thrilled me to no end when students sent me emails with deep thoughts on what we had either discussed in class or they had read for homework.

It disappointed me when they could not point to Canada or Mexico on the map or when they were flabbergasted to learn that Europe and Africa are a jump away from each other.

Then there were those who made me afraid. Who said things like "Let's nuke the hell out of it all—the Middle East, Asia, India." On those evenings, a friend would stay with me on the phone until I reached home, both of us panicky if I had to navigate a poorly lit street.

13

On the night before the start of every new semester, I prepped furiously. I couldn't sleep for more than three hours, wracked as I was by versions of the same nightmare. *What if I opened my mouth and no words of English came out? What if my syllabus was dismissed as "busywork"?* Is there a more terrifying term in American academia than "busywork"? *What if I couldn't provide enough infotainment?*

I imagine that at the beginning of their careers, several of my own capable professors, whether Indian or American, must have had similar fears. Surely they too would have worried about their syllabi, about whether they needed to tweak their lessons or change the method of their delivery. Wise people like my mother, like the senior colleagues I would go to for advice, would assure me that my fears were natural, if not downright welcome. They showed that I cared.

However, my fear about infotainment may have been mine alone. I doubt any of my professors, especially those in India, had ever had to consider the entertainment value of their class. That was a different time, though. Their lives and teaching, their fortunes, didn't depend on ratemyprofessor.com.

14

One semester I joined a university-wide committee. No one paid me, the only untenured adjunct professor, any attention. Still, I showed up to every meeting.

The following semester, I spent back-to-back weekends at a coffee shop downtown, meeting each of my fifty students for one-on-one conferences so we could brainstorm their upcoming assignments.

Every semester, I wrote recommendation letters for every student who asked, for however many institutions or jobs or scholarships they applied to, be it one or five or nine; I collaborated with librarians and faculty members from my department and others; I delivered guest lectures; and I served as an unofficial adviser and mentor for international students. I gave away so much of my time and energy for free, yet I, a brown woman on a predominantly white campus, remained unseen.

I took to doodling Ganesha in the margins of my notebook. I made his elephantine nose rest on his enormous belly; its girth felt the same size as my invisibility. I changed strategies. I quit the grownup committees and joined two student-run clubs as faculty adviser. I immediately felt better. Healed. The students had no time to waste on idle chat. Their energy radiated from their fingertips like fireworks, taking the shape of words and plans they cast out into the universe.

15

Often, in those sixteen semesters, I wondered if I would ever figure out what goes into making a perfect professor. Each year I read the student evaluations carefully. I promised to do better, be better. More smiles. More patience. More encouraging notes.

I did better too, but the process felt discouraging, the path to success nonexistent.

I feel foolish now when I look back at that time. How little I valued my labor and myself. Did I really have to attend every meeting? Show up to every departmental event? Why didn't I read my own contract more carefully? See what it said about the exact number of hours I had to give to my job so I could save for myself my weekends? Why did I go so over and above what was asked of an adjunct, knowing full well that summer was just around the corner, that for nearly four months there would be no pay and I would have to live off my savings? What was the point of it all if there was no way to advance? If there wasn't even the crumb of a teaching award? I had won one as a grad student, after two of my students had nominated me, and that had been deeply meaningful.

What I earned the most was learning about people. When a Catholic student heard that I neither attended church nor had found

Jesus, she began emailing me regularly, telling me how she had been praying for my soul. Each time, she signed off with "Blessings."

Another student insisted he could only concentrate in class when he blasted music through the headphone plugged into his left ear.

Yet another insisted his absence should be excused because his grandmother had died. I conveyed my condolences and granted him extra time to finish his assignment. A week later, he emailed again, insisting he be given two extra weeks because his roommate had shot himself. I scanned the local newspaper. I found nothing. Still, I wrote back, telling him that in the interest of being fair to all my students, I would consider his request if he would send me some proof. He never replied. Weeks later, I learned from a colleague that he had left town, and possibly the university too, because he was on the run.

Day after day I simply returned to the classroom, hoping, believing, knowing that I was not the most boring professor in the world.

FORTY DAYS IN ITALY

IT'S THE LAST DAYS of May in 2017, and I am on my way to Rome. My mind fills up with images of Italy that I have accumulated over the years, thanks to books, movies, and TV shows: olive trees with their skinny arms reaching for the sky, a bowl full of lemons idling on a cheerful dining table, red Vespas parked under stone archways, fashionable men and women walking arm in arm, cathedrals with massive domes overlooking cobblestone streets, the Colosseum, platters stacked with pizzas, slow-moving gondolas (never mind that I will be nowhere near one), and, of course, inspiring speeches by our one true hero and gladiator, Russell Crowe.

I don't want to admit it, but I am also terrified. It's a new country and new continent for me. Sure, I have watched videos and read books in preparation, but the *idea* of a country versus *the lived experience of it* are two different things. When I arrived in the US in 2006, TV had almost led me to believe that every American was deeply in love with Paris Hilton. Perhaps it's my fault and a limitation of my social circle that in all these years of living here, I have yet to meet someone who belongs to this particular demographic.

Once I land in Rome, I will be met by my hosts and a couple of dozen students flying in from all over the US. Together we will board a bus that will take us two hours north, to the medieval city of Viterbo. The students will enroll in a variety of courses, including the one I am teaching on travel writing. Barring occasional field trips, classes will be held at the University of Tuscia.

From the YouTube videos I have watched and the orientation literature I have read, "charming" seems too small and limiting a word to describe Viterbo. Apparently one walks everywhere and the University of Tuscia's campus lies just outside the walls that were built in the eleventh and twelfth centuries. The oldest church dates back to the eighth century CE. The population is small, around 60,000, and unlike folks in big cities like Rome and Milan, most here don't speak English.

ALL THROUGH MY FLIGHTS—from Seattle to Washington, DC, and then to Rome—my mind has been flitting back to a conversation I had with a colleague a year ago. She had taught at a similar program in Greece. Having known each other for years, we had always been friendly and cordial. When she returned from Greece, I sent her an email inviting her to coffee. I wanted to hear all about her travels and teaching experiences.

On the appointed day, once we sat down with our respective beverages, I beamed. "Tell me everything. What you ate, where you stayed, what you checked out. What fun to be able to teach your subject but all the way in beautiful Greece!"

From my standpoint, my companion led a charmed, enviable life. She was married with no kids, she made at least twice my salary, and both she and her husband were tenured professors at our university. On social media, her posts alternated between pictures of travels with friends and whatever cause she was fighting for in the moment, her ever-changing profile picture a mirror of her latest interest. Personally, though, I admired her devotion to students—that I had gotten to witness firsthand over the years—and how often she volunteered for events on campus.

When I asked my question, I was not prepared for her long sigh and the sad shake of her head.

"It really wasn't what I expected," she said. "I now know how useless and invisible you must feel as an adjunct. Nobody knows you or sees you. Nobody cares if you do good work. That's how awful it was for me in Greece. Nobody cared about anything I did."

I don't remember the rest of our conversation. Did we order refills? Did I make an excuse and leave? Did she maybe, eventually, extend a compliment toward Greece or its food or people? Or say something encouraging to me? I can't remember. All I remember is how small and useless her words made me feel, how I wished I had never invited her out to coffee.

I buried that conversation when a few months later, a friend encouraged me to apply for this teaching gig in Italy, when that application got accepted and I began working on the syllabus and assignments, when I watched Rick Steves's videos for preparation and read Anthony Doerr's memoir *Four Seasons in Rome*.

But the conversation, and questions about my worth, resurfaced when the time came to apply for my Italian visa. Because I do not hold an American passport, the steps to acquiring said visa were many and complicated. I had to show details of my bank account, alongside evidence that I was gainfully employed and had compelling reasons to return to the US. I also had to provide the address of where I would stay during my time in Italy, details of what I would teach, for how long, and where. From Idaho, the nearest consulate for me was in San Francisco, a journey of two flights and much shuffling around of my teaching schedule because the trip for the visa had to be made in the middle of the spring semester. My first time at the consulate, the interview lasted less than a minute and my application got rejected. Apparently, one of the documents the agency had provided me with was not the one I needed. A month later, buoyed by renewed vigor, reinforced documents, and about 300 more emails, I tried again. This time I succeeded.

MINUTES FROM LANDING at Rome's Leonardo Da Vinci–Fiumicino Airport, like a poorly buffering video, my mind replayed that conversation with my colleague over and over again. Was her tactlessness a deliberate act of cruelty? I couldn't be sure. It was a sunshine-filled morning, however, and I was where I was supposed to be for the next forty days. But what if, despite the planning and preparation, this all went wrong? What if no one cared? What if, I remained, as my colleague said, "useless and invisible"?

ON THE GROUND, Viterbo is exactly like its pictures and videos have promised. Flower baskets hang from nooks and balconies. Cathedrals loom tall every few feet. Cafés with both indoor and outdoor seating serve a steady stream of cappuccinos, cakes, and pastries, plus savory baked goods dotted with sunshine-yellow zucchini flowers for garnish. One can purchase unlawful quantities of pistachio gelato from practically any gelateria in the city. Or stuff one's face with the saltiest olives and the richest prosciutto. At mealtimes, it's impossible to decide where to eat because walking past every pizzeria and restaurant makes me hungry.

On my second day in Viterbo, my hosts escort me to my apartment, give me a brief tour, and teach me how to operate the washing machine. The one-bedroom space comes with a balcony and wide-open windows. It sits in the heart of the city, in a street lined with restaurants, gelaterias, and shops that sell expensive cosmetics and leather goods. It will take me fifteen minutes to walk to campus through cobblestone streets that I quickly realize look great only on television screens. In real life, they can be hard to walk on, especially if it has been raining and the stones have turned slick, or if the sun is beating down on you, which during summer in Viterbo is every day.

As soon as my hosts leave, I turn off the air conditioner and open all the windows. There is a nice breeze outside, so why not? In the afternoon, when it's time to leave for campus, I double-check to make sure I have locked the main door, but I don't bother to close the windows. Unwittingly, this single act lets in the entire mosquito population of Viterbo. They flock to my apartment and make themselves comfortable, and over the next few days they feast on me with the commitment of someone discovering the magic of, say, pizza for the first time, and for now and forever refusing to eat anything else.

CONTRARY TO MY FIRST IMPRESSION of Viterbo and all that I had been led to believe through films, travel and food shows on TV, and anecdotes from happy tourists, my first few days in Italy are nothing short of miserable. I am the only visiting professor this summer semester, meaning that my colleagues—the other professors—are locals. They have homes and families to return to as soon as they finish teaching. They have worked with each other for years, and understandably, on field trips, they hang out together. When I join them, they helpfully switch from Italian to English to accommodate me, but every few seconds they lapse back into Italian. They are not doing so to be rude. They simply can't help it. I know this from my own experience as a speaker of multiple languages: when you are used to talking to someone in a particular language, it's painful and awkward to switch into another language with them. Your natural instinct, as soon as you make eye contact, is to revert to how you have always communicated with them. To force your brain and tongue to behave differently, to switch gears and grammar, is a big ask. It weighs down the conversation, makes it cumbersome and stilted, and during every lunch or dinner I share with my colleagues, it galls me that I am the reason for their discomfort.

Outside the campus, the locals seem quiet and aloof. Everyone smokes. Or so it seems. The American students, who arrived in Viterbo from cities as diverse as Las Vegas and Amherst, understandably form their own cliques. None of them is outright rude, but barring two young women who chat with me whenever we run into each other, the others keep their distance. I can't blame them. I would have done the same. Correction: I *did* do the same, back when I was their age and went on college trips with friends and a professor or two in charge of all of us. Even if I had had the inclination to talk to the professors, I wouldn't have. I would have held back, convinced that I would be disturbing them and wasting their time. Surely they were reveling in the silence, in taking long walks by themselves and cooking up serious, professorial things inside their heads. It would have exploded my mind if someone had said, "Do you think they could be lonely? Maybe missing their homes and families?"

"No way," I would have said. "They are professors. They have got everything figured out!"

FOR THE FIRST TIME IN MY LIFE, I am lonely in a way I have never been. Not in the twelve years I have thus far lived in the US, not when I have gone for research trips to Canada and Bangladesh, and not when I moved away from my hometown New Delhi to work in Chandigarh, a city five hours away.

I am not unhappy in Viterbo because May and June are unforgivably hot. Nor because on three separate occasions, three men, each a stranger, kisses me on my cheek without an invitation to do so on my part, and one even follows me home, reminding me of the inappropriate and sometimes dangerous attention I received during my teen and young adult years growing up in New Delhi.

Nor am I unhappy in Viterbo because of the two different times I am stopped by restaurant managers as I am about to enter their premises and our conversations go somewhat like this:

What do you want?

Lunch.

No, no. No refugees. No soliciting.

I am not a refugee. I can pay, I reply quickly, tapping my purse.

It stings to say that, to remove from myself so quickly the tag "refugee," knowing that my grandparents on both sides had been refugees once, in India in 1947 soon after Independence and the resulting Partition. When I was growing up, I heard innumerable stories from them of their hunger and rootlessness in those initial months and years, when they were in their twenties. That devastation continued to manifest itself in small and large ways, long after they had successfully reestablished themselves and become parents and then grandparents. For example, none of them could tolerate wastefulness, whether of money or a grain of rice. They were still haunted by memories of the hunger and helplessness they had had to endure.

I, on the other hand, am unhappy in Viterbo for one reason alone, and that is my inability to speak Italian.

When I am not on field trips or teaching, but exploring the city on my own, it is apparent that in restaurant after restaurant, café after café, in plazas, and museums, the unwritten rule of existence is *companionship*. In the US I do a lot of things independently despite the presence of a husband and friends. I go on vacations, writing retreats, and conferences; I read, write, and grade papers by myself in coffee shops; I eat at restaurants; I go see indie movies. I never feel alone. In the US there are always others like me—independent, self-contained islands. Underlying it all, is of course, the role of language. I understand the background chatter. In restaurants and cafés, I recognize what other customers want to eat and drink. Inside bookstores, I can process the titles they are looking to buy. At parks, I can chuckle at the warnings they issue to their children.

In Viterbo, on the other hand, I watch the world through a veil. Grandmothers with little ones under their watch, grandfathers smoking at the plaza, teenagers gathered on the steps of the city's numerous fountains, identically dressed sisters chortling over coffee, large families lingering over Sunday lunch—everything feels filtered, held an arm's distance away. Not only is language a barrier; it also seems no one is ever alone, except for me—a brown woman with curly hair—and the brown men from different countries of Africa. They patrol the city, rolls of socks in their hands and stuffed into shoulder bags, this door-to-door hawking their only source of income. Time and again, I notice locals hurrying past them, pretending not to see them or hear their calls. I do the same. I too ignore them and avoid eye contact. Yet I feel a sense of kinship. Like them, I too am invisible.

THINGS CHANGE, as they are bound to change in any story about travel. Sometime in my second week in Viterbo, I discover a coffee shop named Happiness Café, and soon it's where I walk to every morning for breakfast and a few hours of uninterrupted writing. Some afternoons it's where I meet my seven students for class. On days when I have been visiting museums and art galleries, and otherwise gallivanting about town, I show up in the evenings for a glass of wine and a little something to go with it. The owner-manager has sharp features and beautiful blond hair that she eases into an impeccable chignon every day, and between her no-English and my fifteen-words-of-Italian, we get along fine.

One morning, just as I have sunk my eyes into my laptop, taken several sips of coffee, and I am about to start preparing for that afternoon's lecture, it dawns on me afresh: I'm the first woman in my family to visit Italy, to be so far from home, and amid people who don't look a stitch like me. I am overcome by the privilege of the moment.

My mind takes me to my great-grandmother, Basanta Kumari, a woman I never met and yet someone I think of often. She died in 1969, ten years before my birth. The handful of things I know about her are all based on what others have told me about her. She came from an impoverished family. She was married off to my great-grandfather when she was ten years old. Some of her new family members called her an "old hag," because the norm among upper-caste Bengalis back then was to marry their daughters off when they were nine years old.

I wonder what she would have made of her life if she'd had the same opportunities as me. If she too could have sat by a flower-lined stone staircase, sipping hot coffee that someone else made for her, reading fluently in a language that she wasn't born to, scribbling notes in the margin with the sole purpose of engaging seven twenty-somethings, knowing, at the end of the day, that she gazed outside of herself because she could, that she had played a role in expanding her world and those of others in her care. What a treat it had been to take my students to the Church of San Sisto, the oldest such building in the city, conveniently located next to Porta Romana, the point of entry for centuries of visitors and pilgrims. What an unbelievable honor it was to write inside our classroom at the University of Tuscia, the building itself dating back to the thirteenth century and having served, impossibly, as both a monastery and a prison.

LOOKING BACK, it's clear to me now that finding that café was my first lucky break. It situated me in a way that nothing else had. It gave me the boost I needed to make friends out of my colleagues.

I did it aggressively and relentlessly, reminding myself that I had done this before. I began following up every time someone said, "We should get coffee." I texted anytime anyone gave me their cell phone number. Once, in desperation, I asked the curator of a small museum if she would like to meet me the next day—anytime she liked, morning, afternoon, or evening—for a meal. She looked flabbergasted, then shook her head. Her "no" was polite but firm. I felt foolish then; I feel bad for her now. Her only crime had been to smile and welcome me into the museum in her broken English, and I had seized onto that, her five words my lifejacket.

Soon I began receiving invitations to my colleagues' homes. Perhaps it wasn't so much my aggressive friend-making that worked. It was their large-heartedness. They saw my loneliness and reached out to correct it.

They fed me elaborate meals; tasked me to slice tomatoes, eggplants, and zucchini with them in their colorful kitchens; took me grocery shopping; taught me to distinguish between different kinds of pasta; gifted me fresh produce from their gardens; gave me tours of their orchards of olives and hazelnuts; helped me buy presents for my family; sent me home with bottles of olive oil; and let me play with their children.

In the end, it doesn't matter so much what led to this moment, but it is what I most return to when I remember my time in Viterbo: it's a Saturday afternoon. My colleague-turned-friend Maria has swung by my apartment and picked me up. We drive up to her home. As she pulls into the driveway, I notice the welcome committee gathered at the front door: Maria's children—a little girl and her younger brother—holding hands. Standing behind them is their dad, smiling and keeping an eye on the road.

Maria waves at the assembly. She says to me conspiratorially, "The kids have been waiting for you all morning! They can't believe you don't speak Italian."

I giggle, delighted by their wonder that there can be adults in this world so strange and incompetent they don't know how to speak the one language everyone is *obviously* supposed to know. It reminds me of when I was six years old and I learned for the first time that not every person in the world eats rice and fish curry for lunch. That disbelief stayed with me for days.

Yet at Maria's home, despite my obvious incompetence, we make it work. First we dig into the elaborate lunch she has prepared: melons with prosciutto, homemade bread, salad with ingredients picked fresh from the garden, a warm pasta made from scratch. For dessert, panna cotta with raspberries. For anyone wanting more, a platter full of apricots and watermelons. Our conversation spans food, and school, and life in India versus Italy versus the United States.

After lunch the kids bring me their drawing books. I *ooh* and *aah* at nearly every picture. Sometimes I mix it up and offer enthusiastic high fives instead. Turns out that that is pretty much all we need to communicate, to see and be seen, and, later, for me to be led by little hands on a tour of the garden.

THE CHURCH OF
SANTA MARIA NUOVA

VITERBO, ITALY
June 8, 2017

I enter the Church of Santa Maria Nuova armed with a sketchpad, a recently purchased 2B pencil, and nervousness. I don't know what my professor, the artist Justin Bradshaw, has in mind. That his work is routinely exhibited at galleries in Rome, and our classroom for today is this ancient church, in a foreign city and culture where I have only spent ten days so far, adds to the heft of the moment. I haven't been in a drawing class since I was thirteen, and that was over twenty years ago. I have doodled, yes. In the margins of notebooks, receipts, and writing pads, I have drawn professors, bosses, and colleagues in love with their own voices; old women admonishing young women in restaurants; bored frogs; fish with cigars in their mouths; my husband cooking with every gadget we have ever owned; and, for my brother, scenes from our childhood, where I, the older sister, have always emerged the hero.

Yet here I am now, enrolled in a drawing class because that is an unexpected perk of teaching where I am in Italy: I get to take a class myself. I dutifully scanned the options and chose Drawing and Painting Italy 1.

At first glance, the Church of Santa Maria Nuova seems modest, both in size and ambition, unlike the cathedral in Orvieto that I visited last week. That one, with its detailed mosaics, rose window, bas-reliefs, and bronze doors, had shot up from the earth like it was issuing a challenge to the gods, daring them to look away. In its size and scope, it had reminded me of lavish Hindu temples back home in India that seemed to say the same thing to the puny humans jostling to enter through their gates: "Come on, look up. Here's your chance to lock eyes with the gods."

Thanks to thick stone walls, the interior of Santa Maria Nuova is cool compared to the brutal heat outside. It smells damp, a little earthy, as if our class has accidentally chanced upon a shady, wooded spot in the middle of a desert. Although I am a child of the tropics—I was born in Kolkata and raised in New Delhi—I am not happy in Viterbo's 35-degree Celsius temperature. I have gotten used to living in Idaho, and its annual snows and ice have taught me to forget the roasting temperatures I had once accepted as an unalterable reality of my life.

The interior walls of the church are covered with frescoes. Sure, their colors have faded over time, but their subjects remain easily recognizable. The first thing Justin does is assign each student their "own" fresco. He tells us the frescoes date back to the fifteenth century, although the church itself is older by another 500 years.

"My" fresco closely resembles others I have seen thus far in Italy: Christ on the cross, his arms outstretched, face set in piety, upper body bare, and the lower half draped in sparse white fabric. He is flanked on each side by two figures. A devotee rests at his feet, while two angels hover close to his head.

When Justin points to my fresco and says, "Draw that," my jaw drops. Did I hear him right? Did he actually say, "Draw that?"

I need him to understand that the last time I drew anything was back in the eighth grade. Art, music, physical education—all courses deemed "unnecessary" by our school—were discontinued from the ninth grade onward, lest the three hours a week we spent on these "extracurriculars" prevented us from dedicatedly pursuing subjects deemed more "serious" and therefore more "worthy."

"Please," I want to tell Justin, "I have not come to Viterbo because I have stumbled upon a great, new calling. I am not here to give up a life of writing and transform myself into an artist. I am here to teach Travel Writing. You and I are colleagues at the same institute. I am not a traditional student you can intimidate. I am only taking this class for fun. Come on! You and I have even shared a few coffees and meals. Surely you can't command me to draw crucified Jesus and his friends on the second day of class."

Of course, what I say to him is more along the lines of "Justin, please have mercy."

Justin chuckles. He moves closer to the fresco and breaks the complicated painting down into recognizable shapes. I follow the movement of his right index finger as it jabs the air. "See the heads and the halos? Those are circles. Look at the shape of the bodies. Oblong. Where is Christ standing? On a rectangle. These are not unfamiliar shapes. You know them."

I bite my lip as my mind races to come up with excuses. But Justin's right. Now that he's shown me the shapes, it's impossible not to see them. Still, my hand hesitates over my sketchpad. I write thousands of words every month and think nothing of deleting old drafts. I "kill my darlings" all the time. But this, this act of putting pencil to paper and drawing the first circle, this freezes me.

I move closer to really study my fresco. If you exclude the angels, it comprises six figures in all, two of whom are female. The first is the Virgin Mary. Just like other representations I have seen of her in Italy thus far, here she looks pious. She has covered her head. Her eyes are only for her son, and they are filled with adoration for him. We, the audience, are not her priority.

The other female figure is Santa Barbara, after whom "our" church is named. She is a seventh-century saint. Her eyes are squarely on us, on me, and her gaze unflinching. In that moment I am transported out of this small, quiet church in this small Italian city to halfway across the world, to the bustling port city of Chittagong in Bangladesh. Chittagong is several times the size and population of Viterbo, but, like Viterbo, Chittagong is hot and sweaty in the summer, so it always feels like you are walking through a warm shower. I remember that feeling well, from my visit nine years ago, when I went to Chittagong to research the branch of my family that chose not to migrate to India after the bloody and violent Partition of 1947, opting instead to stay behind.

I REMEMBER HOW on the eve of that trip, I had felt good about visiting Bangladesh. I was going to stay with extended family. I was fluent in Bengali, my mother tongue and the national language of Bangladesh, so I would not have to learn a new language. I would eat deeply familiar foods. Even outside of family, I would surely be able to take pictures and interview folks without any hassle. I would fit right in because I would look like everyone else. Nobody would be able to tell me apart from the locals, unlike in Moscow, Idaho, where I stood out, where it felt like I was one of forty or so brown people in a town of 23,000. In Idaho, everything about me gave away my "foreigner" status—my accent, my questions (*What is Black Friday?*), my preference for food with a minimum of five spices. In Bangladesh, I was going to be just fine.

That illusion shattered the very first day. As soon as I walked into a bookstore, the salesperson asked, "When did you arrive from India?" I mumbled an answer while surreptitiously patting my clothes. What was it? Was there something on my face? What gave me away?

This went on the entire duration of my stay. Every time I entered a store or someone's home, even before I could open my mouth and introduce myself, they would greet me with the same identical question: "When did you arrive from India?"

One evening, while my aunt was putting dinner together, and I was watching her add the finishing touches to shutki, a dried fish delicacy, I asked, "How do they always know I am not from here? What do I do differently from all of you?"

My aunt gathered two handfuls of chopped cilantro, or coriander as we call it in that part of the world, and added them to the simmering gravy. She gave the resulting goodness a stir and laughed, "Because you look them in the eye, silly girl."

"Where else am I supposed to look?"

She shrugged. "At the floor. At the person if you so choose. I don't know. But women here don't look at others with the straight, frank gaze you have. That's all Indian."

It stunned me that it was my eyes that gave me away. Not their color or their shape, but the way they engaged with the world. The irony of it was not lost on me. Whereas in the US, I often had to answer patronizing questions about the state of women in India, with the speaker making it abundantly clear that they thought my best life was unpacking now that I was in America, in Bangladesh it was the exact opposite. Here I, the citizen of a powerful neighboring country, had the self-assured gaze to match it.

BACK IN VITERBO, on that first day inside the Church of Santa Maria Nuova, our class spent close to two hours sketching. Sure, my Mary did not look pious, nor did my Santa Barbara possess an unflinching gaze, and my lopsided Christ ended up with an arm alarmingly longer than the other. Still, it felt good to finish the assignment.

Later that evening, inside the one-bedroom apartment the institute had allotted me, I fixed myself dinner—salty olives, salumi, and crusty bread from a store in my neighborhood, and a glass of red wine. Then I sat at the dining table, opened my laptop, and looked up the life story of Santa Barbara, she, the seventh-century saint and possessor of the powerful gaze.

Born to a wealthy family, she was raised by a loving but overprotective father. He kept her locked in a tower, Rapunzel-like, hidden from the world outside. The more I read about him, the more he reminded me of another overprotective father: King Suddhodhana, the father of Prince Siddhartha, the future Buddha.

At the time of Siddhartha's birth, seers had prophesized that upon reaching maturity, the child would become either a world conqueror or a world renouncer. Needless to say, Suddhodhana wanted his son to conquer the world. So he filled Siddhartha's life with cheerful distractions and eliminated all possible sources of sorrow. He employed runners to ensure that the roads of his kingdom were always clear of the old, sick, and dying. Every time Siddhartha rode out in his carriage, the only daily details he saw were pleasant, perhaps even ordinary.

Yet despite Suddhodana's efforts, one night things didn't go as planned. There were no runners on duty, and Siddhartha saw the very sights—old age, sickness, and death—his father had prevented him from seeing thus far. Distraught, he forsook his home, his princely duties, his young wife and baby son, and set out in search of Enlightenment. Even after he found it and transformed from Prince Siddhartha to Gautama Buddha, he never returned home.

IT MIGHT HAVE BEEN my mother who first asked me to consider, "What if Siddhartha had been a woman? Would he have been able to slink out in the middle of the night, forsake his home and family, and set out in search of Enlightenment? What if his wife Yashodhara had done what he did?"

I was probably twelve years old at that time, and I remember being struck by the question, by the possibilities it opened up, and how it wobbled whatever illusion of fairness and equality I had until then. Was it at all possible? A major world religion founded by a woman? What would that even look like?

Although there is no way to say this with certainty, I think I can make an educated guess about what *would* have happened to Yashodhara if she, instead of Siddhartha, had indeed been the one to leave home. I believe runners and soldiers would have been sent after her. She would have been either killed or dragged back to the palace and confined to a life strictly indoors. How dare she dishonor her family? How dare she forsake her duties as a wife and mother?

What did Yashodhara make of her husband's quest? Why had I never been taught to even consider her side of the story?

WHEN SANTA BARBARA confessed to her father that she had embraced Christianity, he had her imprisoned, tortured, and eventually beheaded. Legend has it that for as long as she lived, she performed miracles. Even after her burial, they continued being reported from the site of her tomb. Isn't it ironical that, though regarded as the patron saint of engineers and mathematicians, Santa Barbara failed herself? She could neither devise an escape nor design a contraption that would protect her from her father, from his love and, ultimately, his sense of right and wrong.

DURING MY FORTY DAYS IN VITERBO, I returned to the church several times just to stare at Santa Barbara. I learned from Justin that she might not have been a part of the original fresco, and might have been a later addition. Some afternoons the church would be busy with tourists; on other days I'd be the only one. Once I addressed her in my head: *Why are you staring at us? Was this the artist's way of granting you agency? Are you holding us all accountable?* I wondered if martyrdom was something she had never even considered. After all, she was a young girl. What if she had only wanted to push back *a little* against the rules established by her father but somehow her intent got lost in translation? What if, instead of asking her for miracles, someone had asked her for a story instead? *Who are you? No, not what you can do for us. Tell us who you are. Who do you want to be?*

The questions shot through my mind because of Santa Barbara, but they stayed with me all through my time in Italy. I visited several churches, museums, and art galleries. I went to Florence, Rome, and Siena. Yes, I was awed by the scale, historicity, and imagination of the builders and the artists. But even to my untrained-in-Italian-art eye, it was apparent that there were few roles available to women outside of saints, virgins, mothers, or, at the other end of the spectrum, Mary Magdalene. The point of view, gaze, execution—they were all Masculine. There was adoration to the point of obsession with heavenly subjects and comparatively scant interest in the earthly or the secular, in anything that might be considered Feminine.

It made me realize yet another reason I so cherish the paintings made in India during the Mughal period. Rooted in Persian miniatures, they flourished between the sixteenth and eighteenth centuries and depict, to my eye, a far wider scope and conceit. They include scenes of hunting, courtship, weddings and processions, combats, tournaments, royal courts. Women appear—by themselves, with their female companions, with birds. They can be seen dressing their hair, drinking from cups, idling in gardens, in royal portraits, and playing musical instruments. I am drawn to them, of course, by familiarity, since my hometown Delhi was the Mughal capital for centuries. I studied the dynasty, especially their contributions in art and architecture, so much so that my first graduate degree was in Mughal history. But beyond that I am fascinated by the stories these paintings tell.

Sure, they do not depict everyone in society, nor do they create heaven on earth. But they show that there is much to be appreciated in this earthly lifetime. Most importantly, they show women's stories. Women laughing, flirting, fulfilling a bunch of roles, and taking as much delight in enjoying music as in watching two elephants lock their tusks. They help me imagine that on the morning she discovered her husband had left her and their young son, Yashodhara considered the vast amount of work to be done, but instead of getting to it immediately, she sat yogi-style in her favorite corner of the room, the one replete with sunshine and cushions. She pulled her heavy tanpura toward herself and laid its long neck across her lap. She adjusted her back, plucked at the strings. Then she closed her eyes and played one imperfect yet satisfying note.

VALENTINE'S DAY

A Fourteen-Point Meditation on Love
and Other Fiery Monsters

1

I MET MY HUSBAND when we were both students at the University
of Idaho. In the fifteen years we have been together thus far, despite
a few half-hearted attempts, his handsomeness, and my attention
to pop culture, Valentine's Day has not become our "thing." If we
remember the date and it happens to be a weekday, we splurge on
chocolates or a nice meal at a restaurant (breakfast or lunch, because
we are not made of money and because dinner reservations for that
night must be made five months in advance, which neither of us
ever remembers to do).

Back when we lived in Idaho, if Valentine's Day fell on a weekend, we sometimes made the 90-to-100-minute drive to the nearest
big city, Spokane, Washington, from our then-hometown of Moscow. We checked ourselves into a nice hotel downtown, namely, the
Spokane Club, which began its life in 1890 as a historic "gentlemen's

club." The first such clubs were set up in eighteenth-century Britain by upper-class men, and they were not accommodating in the least when it came to the gender, race, or social status of their members. Meaning, back when it opened its doors, neither my husband nor I would have been admitted inside the Spokane Club on account of our race, and, in my case, my gender as well.

As guests in the twenty-first century, though, we took great joy in strolling through its august corridors, in whiling away entire afternoons playing Scrabble across marble-topped tables, and in clicking selfies while ghosts of long-dead white men glowered down at us from sepia photographs and grand old paintings.

"Look at those monsters," I imagined them hissing to each other, as they fumed at our insolence, at our metaphorical middle fingers pointed toward them, at their loss of everything that was once good and pure and right.

2

The year I turned twenty-two, I wrote an article about Valentine's Day. From my pulpit of recently gained adulthood, know-it-all-ness, and heightened righteousness, I called it silly and pointless. To my absolute delight, one of the biggest dailies in the country, *The Pioneer*, published it in their New Delhi edition.

The morning it came out, I dutifully scanned it and emailed it to my then-boyfriend, a PhD student at Ohio State University. He loved it and emailed me a dozen sappy e-cards.

I bristled a tiny bit at the irony and at my own hypocrisy. But the cards felt real and the romance everlasting. After all, he had spent so much time picking (and clicking "send"). How lucky was I to have found this perfect man?

Thirteen months later, we broke up. It took fewer than three clicks to delete his emails and cards.

3

In India, Valentine's Day wasn't really a thing until the mid-1990s, when I was a teenager. Sure, it was still the country of the Taj Mahal and the *Kama Sutra*, but in cinema as in real life, romance often assumed prudish forms. I suppose one could say things had improved from how they used to be in the '60s, when my parents were kids. Back then, in Hindi films, two flowers smacking into one another meant, well, you-know-what.

Fast forward twenty to thirty years later to when I was growing up. Now, seduction played out on the screen against the backdrop of heavy rains and a smoldering fire. This fire was everything. It could be in the room, forest, or barn, wherever the boy and girl happened to be. Either they chased each other around it, or they danced facing it, or the camera zoomed into the orange-red flames, indicating that all manners of love were about to be consummated.

4

In the mid-1990s, India underwent a significant change when it opened its doors to economic liberalization. Now American goods and services flooded our markets—chips, sodas, television channels, programs, lifestyle. We rushed to consume them. We all wanted to be cooler and hipper—that is, American.

That's when Valentine's Day entered our lives. With baby steps, hesitant at first. And then, with every passing year, it kept getting bigger, stronger, and hungrier, and so did its demands.

The first to give in to this toddler's tantrums were the roses. In India, we have always had a keen relationship with roses. We love them in our perfumes. We use their extracts in beauty treatments. Their waters scent our desserts, while the dried petals crushed on top serve as an eye-catching garnish. In weddings I attended in my childhood, two kids, usually my age or slightly older, representing the bride's family would flank the entrance and hand out single roses wrapped in foil to each guest as they entered, like they were royal patrons about to grace this occasion with their flower-smelling presence.

Now, because of Valentine's Day, roses popped up for sale everywhere. Fat, juicy, and red, they nodded to us from street corners and traffic lights, inside shiny new malls, outside multiplex theaters, and at the grocer's next to the egg cartons. It was as if we had let red roses take over our city and shame the other flowers to admit defeat and close in on themselves.

5

Or did it begin with the cards?

In New Delhi, if your boyfriend didn't buy you a card from Archie's, the stationery and gift store with multiple locations all over the city, he didn't love you enough. If the card was just regular-sized, he loved you only an average amount. But if it was five times the size of your head, he was going to love you forever.

If you went to my school or college, and on your birthday or on Valentine's Day you strutted around looking smug and determinedly pleased with yourself, it was because you were weighed down by an enormous bouquet and, peeking from within its floral folds, sat an enormous card.

Simply put, you had arrived. You could spend the day basking in the assurance that girls like me who never landed rich boyfriends and who claimed to not care for such ostentatious displays of love and affection would throw (surreptitiously, of course) mad-jealous glances at you, at your bouquet the size of a small ship, and at that coveted card, the map to everything.

6

There were also the balloons—lots and lots of them, red, upbeat, and always heart-shaped.

7

In addition to the cards, the roses, and the balloons, what if your boyfriend also bought you a teddy bear? There was only one answer to this question. This man was a keeper.

8

Because Valentine's Day was such a small thing to begin with, the first protests against it were also on a proportionate scale. The protesters claimed that such open displays of affection were evil Western imports that were destroying Indian values, as if values are tangible, like dry leaves on a fall day, rake-able and toss-able into a fire. Increasingly, however, in a country of more than 1 billion, these protests are neither small nor a laughing matter.

9

Most often, the protesters are conservative men who, for reasons best known to them, feel entrusted and empowered to protect the rest of us from "corrupting Western influences."

i. On the morning of, if they are mildly annoyed with life, they burn cards and tear down celebratory banners.

ii. If they are more peeved than that, they attack flower shops and trample meticulously arranged bouquets beneath their feet.

iii. If they haven't slept well for a few nights in a row, they fan out in search of couples in public places. They accuse them of shaming the country, of dishonoring their respective families, parents, culture, community, and everything else in between.

iv. If they lead truly shitty lives themselves, they vandalize restaurants that seek to profit from this Day of National Shame (*Special Valentine's Day Dinner! Couples Get One Free Appetizer or Dessert of Their Choice!*). They break windows and furniture, throw out celebrating couples, and sometimes carry out their threats of bodily harm.

10

Each year I read about these protests. Each year I wonder, How have these protesters lived until now without knowing about the Sun Temple of Konark? Built in the thirteenth century in the eastern corner of India, the Sun Temple is counted today as a World Heritage Site. But its antiquity alone does not make it unique. It's what's on its walls—detailed, lavish carvings of couples in passionate kisses, embraces, and more, inspired by the *Kama Sutra*, itself written in second-century India.

11

I wonder how these protesters claim to be "expert" Indians without knowing about Kamadeva, our own ancient God of Love. Like Cupid, Kamadeva wields a bow. His is a sugarcane stalk, and the string is made up of honeybees. His arrows are ornamented with five different kinds of flowers—ashoka, blue lotus, white lotus, jasmine, and mango. He prefers the colors yellow and green, symbolic as they are of spring. When he strikes men and women with his special arrows, they have no option but to fall in love.

12

Anywhere in America I happen to be on February 14, I hear about the gifts and cards schoolchildren exchange inside classrooms here. I see magazine covers promising life-changing wisdom such as "33 Ways to Capture Your Man's Heart and More." At our home, my husband takes me out to dinner the next weekend both of us are able to do so. I, in turn, make up stories and handmade cards for him. In these stories, despite his protests, his favorite fictional characters—such as *Star War*'s Yoda, Khaleesi of *Game of Thrones*' fame, and Batman—fall deplorably, and sometimes inappropriately, in love with each other. That entire week, I walk past store windows gloriously trussed up in pink and red before they too must accept defeat and fold in on themselves to make room for the green of St. Patrick's Day.

13

But not once do I pause my celebrations (or the lack thereof) to worry about hapless threatened couples in India.

14

It is only the next morning, while reading the *Times of India*, that I remember them, when I come across headlines such as "Fourteen Cities in India to Celebrate Valentine's Day: Arranged from Least Safe to Most Safe." I look at pictures of destroyed property, of massive bonfires devouring red-hearted cards, of angry mobs shouting slogans and holding up puny flags to save a culture that's thousands of years old, as if it's not robust on its own, as if it needs their saving. I see girls hiding their faces behind scarves to avoid being captured on camera, and the hunched shoulders of their boyfriends accepting their fate with what I assume is a mix of shame and resignation. I wonder why these girls and boys set out to celebrate Valentine's Day in the first place.

I don't dare imagine what happens to girl-girl, boy-boy couples, and to other combinations of falling in love and being in love that still remain mostly invisible in mainstream Indian society. Why do they leave the security of their homes, knowing full well they are courting harassment and perhaps far worse?

Do they do so to be modern Romeos and Juliets and celebrate love for love's sake? Because they foolishly believe they should be allowed to be themselves in their own city and country? Or because they thrill in being monstrously insolent, in sticking metaphorical middle fingers to all those men lamenting the loss of everything that was once good and pure and right?

STRANGER, WONDER, CHICAGO

DECEMBER 2006

From the observation deck of Sears Tower, I can see miles upon miles of Chicago and, lidding it, a gray-orange-red sky. The parallel lines of cars—flashing red and yellow lights—are as busy as the planes taking off from O'Hare, matchsticks really, their sparks missing each other by centimeters. The skyscrapers are pencil stubs—fat, skinny, tall, short—lined together along the skyline. In the ten minutes I've been here, the sky, cars, planes, and skyscrapers have watched me go from heightened elation to crushing despondency.

LET ME BACK UP. Four months ago, in August 2006, when I arrived in Idaho, I did not foresee that a vast and extensive train trip from Spokane, Washington—my nearest train station—to Toronto, Canada, was in my future. I had assumed I would spend my winter holidays broke and alone. My roommate would leave town at the earliest opportunity to be with her boyfriend in Seattle. Other close friends would disappear into the warm homes, embraces, and overstuffed tables of their families near and far.

I would remain in my TV-less apartment, nervous to engage with the still-unfamiliar snow and ice outside, enduring days on end without any meaningful conversation because I owned neither a phone nor a laptop, and missing New Delhi in a way I wouldn't have thought possible. I was caught between the teeth of a giant machine; bit by serrated bit, it was consuming everything I had once taken for granted: a belly full of flavorful food, endless cups of my mother's black tea, telephone calls and dates with countless friends, and TV channels crowded with festive shows and films in Hindi.

My grim view of my first December abroad changed the day my uncle—my father's first cousin—emailed from Toronto. He and his family were thrilled that I was here in North America. Wouldn't I please let him buy me a ticket to visit them? They'd love for me to stay a couple of weeks at least. *The entire duration of your holidays, please, if you can manage it. We want you here,* my uncle wrote.

A month with a beloved aunt and uncle eating homemade, familiar food, speaking in Bengali, taking in a new, foreign city where I would have access to Hindi movies and Indian restaurants—why hesitate? What was there to think about? I replied within seconds.

Yes. Absolutely, yes. Could you buy me train tickets though? I wrote. *I don't want to fly. I want to see as much of North America as possible.*

The next morning, three shiny tickets pinged in my inbox. Amtrak tickets. Spokane to Chicago; Chicago to New York; and finally, New York to Toronto.

BY THE TIME I reached Chicago, I had crossed seven states—Idaho, Washington, Montana, North Dakota, Minnesota, Wisconsin, Illinois—and three time zones. There were four states left before reaching Toronto—Indiana, Ohio, Pennsylvania, and New York. My conversation partners had ranged from Hannah, a singer of Portuguese ballads, to Sam, a Vietnam vet; and Ben, a professional Santa Claus, to Lon, a physician who had visited India many times and knew more about Bangalore than most Bangaloreans.

I was awed by the Rockies, by Montana's skies, and by the dark waters of the Mississippi. From my window, I watched Americans go about their lives as the train passed farms, one-person railway stations, coal mines, churches, factories, cities, and mansions.

Back in Idaho, when I had announced my Amtrak plans to friends and classmates, they had cheered me on with cautious enthusiasm. A few had gone so far as to share horror stories of their own train travels— of running into addicts and drunks and having to deal with horrible toilets and overpriced food. While none of their concerns made me reconsider my plans, their warnings did make me nervous.

When I got off the train in Chicago, I felt triumphant. Vindicated. My journey thus far had been perfect.

BUT THAT WAS HALF AN HOUR AGO. Now, from this 110th floor where planes are the size of matchsticks, cars nothing but dots, and people on the streets below too minuscule to be seen, the universe is telling me something entirely different. It is saying that I don't matter. I never have. I'm puny. Insignificant. No achievement, no glory, no sacrifices made just so I could study abroad would ever amount to anything.

For the first time in America, I am scared. This isn't home; I'm not supposed to be here. Just last week, the receptionist at the student health center on campus had assumed, even before I had opened my mouth, that I wasn't fluent in English. She had yelled instructions and yelled them slowly, word by word. My cheeks had burned from a combination of shame and rage. Homesickness had risen like bile inside me, and jabbing a finger at myself, I had yelled right back.

"Graduate student, creative writing, Department of English, this very university. Your government requires all foreign students to pass a test of English before granting them a visa. Do you want to know my score? A fucking 94 percent. I bet I could teach *you* some English."

I had watched with satisfaction as her face had crumpled, but truth be told, it hadn't taken the sting out of her words or made my day any better.

MY WATCH TELLS ME I have a bit of time to kill before my next train. I look around, at this space teeming with families and tourists in groups, pairs, and singles, and I can't bear to engage with yet another stranger. I want to be home. Seemingly, I have forgotten that my entire trip thus far has been full of kind strangers. We have had to make eye contact, ask what station is approaching next, and look out the same window. Smartphones are a thing of the future. We don't own them yet; we don't even know they exist. We have had to rely on each other, especially at nighttime, when the train is speeding over some vast nameless landscape, and there's nothing to see through the windows or the viewing gallery. What to do, then? Sleep, read, or talk.

Last night, sometime after dinner, when the world outside had turned dark, my seatmate Hannah, the singer of Portuguese ballads, had picked up her guitar. Somehow, even before her fingers had struck the first chord, the compartment had fallen silent, as if in anticipation. Did our fellow passengers know she was about to sing? Did they see her pull her guitar out of its sleeve? Was she a regular on the route, perhaps? I don't know. But I remember how it all felt— the rhythmic motion of the train, the occasional bursts of light from outside, the dim blue light overhead, and Hannah's clear voice singing words I didn't understand but I think they were full of longing.

Was it really a love ballad, as she told me afterward? Or maybe it was an inside joke. A nursery rhyme: an ode to the codfish that she composed in the moment, knowing full well that no one on the train would understand the words.

I TAKE A DEEP BREATH. I don't want to be sad, nor do I want to stay lost inside my own head. I need a distraction. And there he is, standing in the corner, watching. His blazer says he works here. He is in his mid-forties, a clean-shaven Black man. Every time he moves, light bounces off his smooth head. He is easily six-feet-something to my five-foot Indian frame. I want to ask him how he can stand to do this job. How does he not go crazy greeting strangers all day, hearing them *ooh* and *aah* and watching them pose as their camera lights flash off the windows?

"Hi! How can I help you?" He asks as I approach him. His voice and tone are both matter-of-fact.

I don't know how to beat around the bush. "This is probably a weird question: How long have you worked here?"

If he is surprised, he doesn't show it. He doesn't ask me why I need this information. He thinks my question over for a minute and says, "Seven years."

"It's my first time here."

He welcomes me to Chicago and asks where I am from. He points to the name tag on his blazer and says, "I am George."

"I am Sayantani."

"What does it mean? Your name?"

"'Twilight,'" I say, "Sayantani means 'twilight' in Sanskrit."

In companionable silence, George and I take in the view. The planes are still at it, as are the cars. Behind us, the elevator dings open and belches out another mouthful of visitors. They rush to the windows, cameras in hand, the way I had.

"So, George, do you like working here?" I ask.

"Yes, I love it. Why?"

"What do you love about it?"

He shrugs as if the answer is obvious. "I get to see so much of the world."

"Do you ever feel pessimistic? I mean, look at the cars. You can't tell there's anyone inside. Does this make you feel . . . insignificant?" I shut up abruptly. "Insignificant?" What the hell is wrong with me? Why am I trying to make this nice man feel bad about his job?

George doesn't look offended. "No. It makes me realize how big God is."

I want to roll my eyes, but I don't. I've been an atheist since I was fifteen, an agnostic for even longer. My family isn't big on religion, and when I was growing up, there was no insistence on regular trips to temples or on following any rituals. All these years later, I cannot be proselytized on top of Sears Tower, one of the most capitalistic achievements of humankind. "If it works for you," I say. "I'm not a religious person."

"Standing here doesn't make you believe in yourself?"

136

"No."

"Tell me: Have you ever done something that people told you not to do but you did it anyway?"

"Yes," I offer hesitatingly. "Not everyone was enthused about my coming to Idaho. Even this train journey. Quite a few people discouraged me from taking the train."

"Exactly. But you still did those things. You did them because you wanted to. You made them possible."

"What does God have to do with it?"

"You don't see it as God's work. But I do. You followed through on your plans. Not everyone does that."

I can't help but smile at George's sincerity. I can see it in his eyes that he absolutely believes every word of what he is saying. How do you argue with someone who is trying to make you like yourself in a moment when you are finding it hard to do so? "Thanks, George. I am not sure that's how this all works."

George shakes his head and points to the sky. "Do you see that? Do you see those colors?"

I nod. The gray-orange-red sky is impossible to ignore. Chicago sure knows how to serve a grand sunset.

George studies me studying the colors. "That's God's work," he says. "Now, don't go all science and technology on me, lady." His tone softens. "You know how I see God's work in you? There are thousands and thousands of people that come to Sears every day. They come from all over the world. But you're the only one who has stopped to chat with me. And you are telling me you're insignificant? Nope. That's not gonna work," he says firmly, closing down my argument once and for all.

I laugh. For now, his words are enough. They pull me out of something I had walked into, something sinister I wasn't expecting. Is there even a name for it? A clinical term perhaps? There should be one for these most fundamental of human moments, when you go from feeling good about yourself to battling your worst doubts, and all within a spate of a few minutes.

Buoyed by his words, I say goodbye to George. I almost can't believe the interaction we have just had. The ten or so minutes with him feel like they were out of a Hallmark movie and that any moment now, a crescendo of triumphant music will descend on us. Or it will rain, and I will have a meet-cute with a handsome stranger who will turn out to be my soulmate.

I check my watch. I grab a sandwich from the nearest Potbelly sandwich shop and head off to the station. Next stop, New York, and after that, Toronto.

JUNE 2009

It's summer three years later, and I am back in Chicago on the same observation deck. This time I am with my father. Baba has flown here from India on a work trip. I have come, once again, from Idaho. I now teach at the same university where I once was a student. I get along well with my American friends, colleagues, and students. I have a boyfriend, a Sikh man of Indian origin. Born in Toronto, raised in Los Angeles, he met and fell in love with me in Idaho. His parents had migrated from India in the 1980s. But because of where he has lived thus far, he is more American than Indian. He and I have discussed marriage. Who knows? Some day this country might feel wholly mine.

Baba and I are thrilled to be in Chicago together. It's like we are both in Delhi and I am a kid again. And maybe it's a Saturday, and I am tagging along as Baba runs errands all over the city, with stops every now and then to keep me happy. A snack here. A cold drink there. The certainty that we will return home with the purchase of a book or two.

Thus far, in Chicago, Baba and I have had our share of the deep-dish pizza. We have explored numerous museums, including the Field Museum of Natural History, where we specifically went to see the two reconstructed man-eating lions of Tsavo that inspired the 1996 film *The Ghost and the Darkness*. Starring Val Kilmer and Michael Douglas, it had come out when I was still in school, and our entire family had gone to the theaters to watch it.

Now, atop the Sears Tower observation deck, Baba and I slow down. We walk around, marveling at the sights and posing for pictures. Neither of us makes any mention of it, but I am sure we are both thinking the same thing: our time together is fast approaching its end. In just a few days, Baba will return home, and I will be back in Idaho.

The attendant this afternoon is a tall white man with blond hair. I want to know if he knows my old friend George. Perhaps he will chuckle and say, "Oh man, I love George!" or he will ask, "How do *you* know George?" At the very least, I hope he will convey my thanks to George. That December evening three years ago, he could not have known how close I had come to the edge. If there had been a way to jump off this 110th floor, I would have. The Sears exudes an overwhelming sense of power and grandeur. Add to that, this view—the planes, the skyscrapers, the lights. So majestic. How does a broke, homesick student stand up to it? How does she not feel overwhelmed?

The attendant shakes his head. "Sorry," he says. "I've worked here for five years. There is no one named George on our team."

Later, over drinks at the rooftop bar, I tell my father about George, but I don't tell him about my homesickness. Who was he really? A ghost? God? A temporary employee filling in for someone? Or maybe a tourist like me?

Growing up in a city like New Delhi, I have always known to be wary of strangers. My suspicion didn't leave me when I moved to Moscow, where strangers smiled at each other and left their laptops unattended at cafés—things you just didn't do in New Delhi. In a way, it feels like Moscow prepared me to receive George. Yet the irony is, I had to come all the way to Chicago, a city just as crowded and complex as the one in which I was raised, to meet him, the stranger I most needed at that unexpected moment. Perhaps, like me, George too had once been lost in America, but he searched, and found himself under that gray-orange-red sky of Chicago.

NICER IN HINDI

WHEN I FIRST CAME TO the United States, I was surprised by how much I missed the atmospheric soup that is New Delhi. It's the unapologetic buzz of a multilingual city and its daily life—the latest Hindi, English, and Punjabi songs crooning from neighboring homes and shops; bells and calls for prayers from temples and mosques; and conversations in languages as disparate as Urdu, Tamil, and Bengali.

I decided that the only way I could hold on to everything in New Delhi was by keeping an eye out for every movie, song, or even advertisement made in the language I missed the most, Hindi. I was going to watch it all, so that when I returned, whether after a year or three, I would slide right back to where things were when I left. No one, friends or family, would be able to tell that I was ever gone from the country.

Through the entirety of that first semester, on afternoons when I didn't have classes or homework, I would check out a laptop from the campus library, plug in my headphones, and search for every Hindi song and movie just released in India. This was how I was going to hold on with all my might, resisting and defying the forces of change.

HINDI ENTERED MY LIFE when I was five years old and my parents and I moved from Kolkata to New Delhi. At home we still spoke Bengali, but since Hindi was the primary language of our new city, I was now required to learn it quickly. Bengali and Hindi are both derived from Sanskrit, so one might think that if you already know one, you might pick up the other with ease, especially since they share a few identical-looking letters. But that is not the case. Sure, the two languages have a few words in common, but for the most part, they *sound* different, and they have their own unique grammar and script.

For one, Bengali has no gender. Everyone can be described using the same pronouns, whether one's father or mother, teachers, the Catholic nuns at school, or, say, the neighbors who forgot to get you a gift on your last birthday. In Hindi, on the other hand, everything has gender, including, most mystifyingly, buses (feminine) and trucks (masculine).

Bengali contains twenty-eight letters, and Hindi forty-four. I am just starting to figure out these shapes when English is also introduced in my life, shoving twenty-six additional letters into my orbit. Now, there's five-year-old me, and ninety-eight letters I must be able to read and write.

At least they are all written from left to right, so that's one less thing to be confused about.

A few years later, when I am ten, I learn that Bengali and Hindi are the fifth and sixth most spoken languages in the world. I am blown away by this fact. It's funny to me that millions and millions of people in the world apparently say or write the same things as I do. Then who am I? Am I really me, or an echo of all these others?

WHEN I TALK TO MY MOTHER on the phone, my husband insists it sounds like *"Haashe paashe haashe paashe khorororororo."* It makes me giggle, this imitation, this string of nonsense words. Bengali is not one of his languages, but now, after fifteen years together, he has mastered the important stuff. He knows how to swear in Bengali, and how to say, "I am hungry," "This is delicious," and "I must use the bathroom."

My husband speaks to his mother in Punjabi, a language I understand but cannot speak. He usually emerges from these conversations relaxed and smiling. He laughs and exchanges gossip with her, begs for recipes that he loved as a kid and wants to re-create in our kitchen. He teases her when her measurements are vague, when she issues instructions like, "Oh, just throw in a pinch." A day or so later, when he updates her on how the food turned out, it's like I have a window into his childhood. Look, here he is, talking to his first friend, his source for his mother tongue.

AS SOMEONE BORN in a former colony of Britain, my fluency and, dare I say, expertise in English is neither unusual nor unique. There are many others like me. It makes me wonder if I would have felt the same longing for, say, French, Dutch, or Portuguese if India had been thoroughly and absolutely colonized by one of those countries instead. (I wonder about this because it's not as if they didn't try; they just didn't succeed.)

In *A Thousand Years of Good Prayers*, Yiyun Li writes, "English is my private language." When I was growing up, English didn't feel "private" to me, perhaps because I was surrounded by English speakers both in my family and outside. Neither does it feel "private" now when I am surrounded by English speakers every second of my life, including at home, where I speak English with my husband, and at the university, where I teach creative writing.

But yes, the inherent logic of English has always come easily to me. It has given me a sense of ownership that I haven't felt over my other languages.

As a child, I read extensively in Bengali, Hindi, and English. I wrote stories and poems in Hindi and English, the languages I got to practice daily in school.

But somewhere along the way, things changed.

English and Hindi entered a boxing ring. They put on gloves and faced each other. There was no point, though. I already knew the outcome. The game was rigged from the start. Hindi was going to lose, and this is because when I was growing up, the Hindi literature curriculum at school often felt old and cobwebby. There were poems and stories about patriotism and pious gods set in hinterlands, far from any place I knew. On those cruelly hot afternoons, inside classrooms that contained no more than three overhead fans for fifty-plus students, how could I be expected to care for events that had transpired during my grandparents' time or long before? If only I had read a story or two about teenagers growing up in contemporary, urban India instead of men and women twice or thrice my age, living and dying a few generations ago.

Conversely, I hugged my English classes to my chest. English was funny, as in Roald Dahl's short story "The Umbrella Man," about a young girl, her hypocritical mom, and the strange man they encountered on a rainy day. English was scary, as in the excerpt from Juliane Koepcke's memoir *When I Fell from the Sky*, about the eleven days she spent in the Peruvian rainforest after surviving a plane crash that killed everyone on board, including her mother. English was mischievous yet wise, as in Vikram Seth's poem "The Frog and the Nightingale," ostensibly about two singers in a bog but really about ambition and envy.

Recently, on social media, I asked my school friends for their memories of our Hindi classes. Did they remember what I remembered? A few did. One did not. She wrote, "I enjoyed our Hindi literature classes because the background of the stories was always relatable to me. I struggled with some of the English books because I couldn't visualize the countryside and had no idea what the trees looked like."

MY HUSBAND TELLS ME, "You are a nicer person in Hindi than you are in English."

I believe him. For everything that English has granted me, it has also been the language of competition and of getting ahead in life.

It's the language in which I was reprimanded at school, especially if my friends and I were caught speaking to each other in Hindi. "This is an English-medium school," our teachers would say. "Speak in English here." It's the language I used in college, at my universities, and during job interviews. Now in writing books, and teaching creative writing, English is also the source of my daily bread and butter, and of my relationships with Americans. It's the language through which I establish my authority in a classroom, order a cup of coffee, check out books in the library.

Hindi, on the other hand, is the language of my neighborhood crushes. It's what I use to talk to my best friends from childhood. It's the first tool I picked up when I stepped out of my parents' orbit and started school. In fifth grade, when I beat everyone else in my class and got the highest score in Hindi, Baba couldn't stop telling our friends and family about it.

I don't think I quite understood his sentiment then. But I get it now. Baba's pride was related to his relief. Four years ago, it was because of him and his new job that we had been plucked out of Kolkata and I had had to learn this complex new language. And now, here I was, proving that we as a family were okay. That I was okay.

Hindi is also the language of TV shows and films I watched on the first television my parents ever owned. My dad built it from scratch—as a hobby—and named it after my mother. At home, though, Baba insisted we speak only in Bengali. After all, who were we as people if we allowed ourselves to forget our mother tongue?

Halfway across the world from New Delhi, in Los Angeles, my mother-in-law followed the same principle, though maybe she didn't put it in exactly those words. She spoke Punjabi at home, but her sons—my husband is her eldest—succeeded in sneaking in English. She stayed on top of her second language, Hindi, through movies the family rented from local Indian grocery stores. She couldn't have known then that two decades in the future, knowing Hindi was going to come in handy when speaking to me, her daughter-in-law.

SHORTLY AFTER my first three months in the US, I realized that watching every Hindi song and movie and ad was not a sustainable practice. Plus, as Ma said, "You are there now. You must immerse yourself in that life. If you keep looking toward here, you will miss out. And that won't be fair to you or to either of the two places."

Here, instead, are sustainable habits I have devised over time:

1. Every Sunday, when I meal-prep, Hindi films play in the background. Sometimes, even an hour into the film, I would have not looked at the screen or registered the actors or plot. When my husband walks into the kitchen, he might comment along the lines of, "Your back is turned against the TV. How are you watching anything?" I never have a good answer except, "It doesn't matter whether I see them or not. It's my ears that need it."

2. My spice jars are labeled in Bengali or Hindi.

3. If I have had an especially busy week and all my energy has gone into conversing, writing, teaching, and thinking in English, I will spend most of the weekend binge-watching Hindi movies. A cleanse and a reset.

4. I routinely search YouTube for new and old recordings of Hindi poems. When a poem moves me, whether on account of its words or the deft delivery of the reciter, I jot it down, word for word, in a journal I have dedicated to this purpose.

Does the acquisition of language stall at the point of immigration? Perhaps. I know I have not gone further in my study of either Bengali and Hindi, and my fluency has suffered and taken a back seat. In her essay "Mother Tongue," Yoojin Grace Wuertz writes, "I imagine that behind every bilingual person there is a story of separation. Of homes left behind, families divided, identities remade over and over again. A history of loss in addition to the mixed gains of the American Dream."

Cheekily, I want to ask, "What then if you are trilingual?"

IT'S THE WINTER OF 2017, and I am back at my parents' home in New Delhi. I show up at the dining table and food appears magically.

My mother's perfectly blended black tea, a mix of Assamese and Darjeeling leaves, alights in beautiful cups at regular hours of the day. I write every morning, and in the afternoons, I reread books that were childhood favorites. Most evenings, on his way back home from work, my brother surprises me with beloved snacks we used to enjoy as kids. It's a charmed life and I have no complaints.

A month later, my husband joins me. This is his first time visiting my family, and I am confident everyone will get along well with everyone. They all get along with me. Why won't they with each other? Naively, I haven't considered the language barrier even once.

My mother reads and understands English well but sometimes feels hesitant speaking it. My husband's English comes with an American accent. My father switches between English and Bengali, as do I and my brother, to make my husband feel included.

It doesn't work.

Put a roomful of Bengalis or any other linguistic group together and they will switch to their own language despite knowing better and wanting to make the outsider feel included.

Whereas just a few days ago, I had looked forward to my husband's arrival, I now grow resentful. It's because of him I am "forced" to speak in English. He is the reason I must translate continuously. In a matter of days we will return to the US, where once again I will be required to speak English 24/7. Why won't he give me this respite?

More than anything else, I am exhausted from having to constantly translate between two languages. The switch is not just between words, syntax, and grammar. It's of something fundamental and rooted in my core. It's as if I inhabit a different mind and body when I speak Bengali or Hindi than when I speak English. Who is the real me, then? What is her preferred language?

ON A WARM AFTERNOON in July 2018, my husband and I entered a tattoo parlor in downtown Moscow, Idaho. I had made the appointment a week earlier, although I had been considering and rejecting designs for years. I couldn't decide. Should it be the three eyes of Durga, my favorite Hindu goddess? Or the outline of Nautilus, the submarine from Jules Verne's *Twenty Thousand Leagues under the Sea*? Or maybe a tiny map of Delhi?

Finally, once I decided, the tattoo artist—a skinny white guy with tattoos all the way up and down his arms, legs, and neck—placed paper cutouts of my selection at various points of my right arm. Nothing fit, nothing seemed right, until he placed it on my wrist.

"Yes," I said. I had chosen two words, in their distinct scripts: *Golpo* and *Katha*, the Bengali and Hindi words for "story." When the tattooist finished inking, I felt a sweet, if silly, relief. This, right here, was a little reminder, a nudge, that I was still the person I was meant to be. That I was, and will continue to be, in my husband's words, "nicer in Hindi." That no matter how my day went, how much of it I spent speaking English, at night I was still going to dream in Bengali. If ever that changes, I will know that the ninety-eight letters I had once learned to read and write have fallen out of the jigsaw board of my mind and rearranged themselves. I don't know what I will say to myself then or in what language.

JUDITH AND HOLOFERNES

IN THE FALL OF 2019, I receive an email from Helena Feder, the Mellon/ ACLS (American Council of Learned Societies) scholar in residence at the North Carolina Museum of Art. The museum is putting together a book in celebration of its permanent collection. Titled *You Are the River*, it will feature over fifty writers from across North Carolina. Each of us will contribute a story, poem, or essay inspired by an artwork of our choosing.

It takes me less than a day to say yes. When Helena sends me the links to the permanent collection, I choose Kehinde Wiley's *Judith and Holofernes* as soon as it appears on my laptop screen. I am familiar neither with the artist nor with the subject. But I am drawn to this painting because in its use of audacious colors and the emphasis on the subject's eyes, it reminds me of Hindu iconography. I also see evidence of Renaissance-era paintings in the way the artist has set electric blue, yellow, green, and orange flowers against a black backdrop, mimicking the sort of ornate drapes one might call "sumptuous." Unlike most Renaissance-era paintings, however, the subject of this is not the Holy Trinity, or Jesus and his mother, or an enigmatic woman with a secret smile.

Instead, it's a Black woman. She looks to be in her thirties or forties. She is leaning to a side, her jaw set in a line, and her eyes trained on you, the observer. She has a resolute chin and a wide nose. Her thick black hair is gathered on the top of her head like a crown. She has accessorized her off-the-shoulder, royal-blue dress with a leather and metal belt. The artist has captured different shades of blue in how the dress responds to light and shadow. The most striking detail, however, is that just like the Hindu goddess Kali, this woman is holding up a severed head. But unlike Kali, who holds up the head of a demon and in this way represents the destruction of Ignorance and the triumph of Knowledge, this woman is holding up the head of a white woman.

I don't know these two women. I don't know the story that has led them to this end. Before my words can enter any conversation with Wiley's painting, I need to dive into research. I need to learn about Judith and Holofernes.

IF YOU ARE AS UNFAMILIAR with biblical stories as I am, you need a guide. Granted, I attended a Catholic school for twelve years, so I should be more familiar. But listen, I also grew up in New Delhi, which is why my sense of iconography stems mostly from Hinduism, followed by a mishmash of Islam and Sikhism, and then everything else.

The story goes like this. Holofernes, an Assyrian general, invades the Jewish city of Bethulia, on the order of King Nebuchadnezzar. A young widow named Judith swears to kill Holofernes and avenge her people. She possesses extraordinary beauty. That, however, is not the point of this story. At least, not the entire point. Not at this time.

On the appointed day, Judith rises early. She prays and dresses herself in fine clothes. She enters the enemy camp, her mind set, and her eyes in search of Holofernes. When guards stop her, she tells them she is here to help the general. She will reveal secrets about her people so he may win. Except, of course, Judith is no traitor.

Before long, she is approached by an inebriated Holofernes. He does not know her identity, but so captivated is he by her beauty that he absolutely must. Judith encourages him to keep drinking. Finally, when he is stupid drunk, when he can neither stand nor offer resistance, she snatches Holofernes's sword, and beheads him in one fell swoop, thus keeping her word to her people. As the story goes, the severed head is then carried out by one of Judith's servants. With Holofernes gone, the Israelites are easily able to defeat the invaders.

What happens to Judith afterward?

Some glorify her strength. *Really, how does a young woman take on a mighty military commander on her own?* Others praise her virtue. *Look, Judith never took up with another man. After her husband died, she lived as a celibate for the rest of her life.* Still others praise her courage. *Judith is the heroine we need, a true symbol of resistance against tyrants.*

So gripping and unexpected is this story of a young and beautiful widow beheading a powerful man, a warrior no less, and with his own sword, that over and over artists reimagine Judith and Holofernes, on canvas, sculpture, and even the Sistine Chapel.

- Look, here is Judith with an olive branch in her hand, offering it as a symbol of peace, while her maid Abra walks behind her, carrying Holofernes's head on top of her own like it's a fruit basket.

- Now Judith has porcelain-white skin and brown ringlets. She appears calm as Holofernes's head falls into a sack held by her servant.

- This Judith is blond and wears her straight hair in a neat bun.

- That Judith is a Greek goddess, virginal and youthful, draped in loose clothing.

- Now Judith is brunette, and her aggressive stance matches her unruly hair.

- Here Judith is a powerful noblewoman, dressed in a red velvet gown and a jaunty hat with feathers.

• This Judith is nude with her breasts exposed, but her arms and shoulders are muscular like a man's.

Even Holofernes's sword does not remain a sword. In the hands and imaginations of different artists, it switches shapes and forms. Here a cutlass, there a scimitar, now a machete, then a saber.

IT'S WHILE I AM RESEARCHING these different versions that I come across the painting of Judith and Holofernes by Artemisia Gentileschi. She finished painting it in 1620, when she was only nineteen years old.

It's a violent depiction: Holofernes lies on the bed, and Judith has grabbed his hair with her left hand while she pushes down his head. The sword is in her right hand. She has plunged it straight through Holofernes's neck. The blood spurts so profusely it has stained the sheets, it's running down the bed, and it has splattered onto Judith and her maid's arms and dresses. Both the women's faces are dark and focused with concentration. You can see the strain on their arms. The task at hand is no walk in the park after all. I am struck by how convincing the painting seems to me. Unlike in others' depictions, Judith's body here has the power and heft that makes this act of violence believable.

I am no art scholar, but this painting also feels much gorier and more visceral than the others. As it turns out, I am not imagining it. The Uffizi Gallery in Florence, where the painting is currently housed, discusses this on its website:

> The naturalistic "virility" of the work provoked strong reactions on its arrival in Florence and the painting was denied the honor of being exhibited in the Gallery; in fact, it was only with great difficulty and the help of her friend Galileo Galilei that the painter managed to extract the payment. . . . Today, this painting also represents the human and professional tale of a woman who chose to be an artist in an era dominated by men; in this she succeeded, working in the courts of Rome, Florence, and Naples, traveling to England and finally becoming the first woman to enter the Academy of Art and Design in Florence.

Some critics believe that Artemisia offered herself catharsis through this painting. Born in 1593 in Rome, she was the daughter of Orazio Gentileschi, a well-respected painter. Her mother died young, leaving Artemisia in charge of three brothers. As was the practice at the time, she didn't learn to read or write until later in life, but she showed incredible promise as an artist from early childhood. In 1611, when Artemisia was seventeen years old, the artist Agostino Tassi, a friend of her father's, raped her. At that time, because an unwed girl's body was not her own—it was property that belonged to her father—Orazio convinced Artemisia to seek justice.

A public trial was held. Artemisia had to not only provide details of the rape but also undergo an exacting punishment. As Rebecca Mead writes in the essay "A Fuller Picture of Artemisia Gentileschi" in the *New Yorker*, "To insure that rape accusations were truthful, alleged victims were required to submit to a form of torture: cords were wrapped around their hands and tightened like thumbscrews. 'It is true, it is true, it is true,' she repeated as the cords were tightened."

Other critics argue that to equate Artemisia's work with her assault is both reductive and simplistic. There was a lot more to her life and identity, as wife, mother, lover, and artist. Artemisia inhabited all these roles, especially that of an artist, given the significant body of work she created in a career spanning forty years.

IT'S MARCH 2020, and the world is in lockdown, when I reapproach my assignment. My essay is due to the museum in two months. Once more, I plunge into research. I want to learn about Kehinde Wiley. Who is he besides the artist responsible for the official portrait of President Obama that hangs inside the National Portrait Gallery?

Born in Los Angeles in 1977, Wiley studied art at Yale. He paints in what he calls "street style," wherein he approaches strangers on the streets and asks them if they will serve as models. Often he chooses both the model's pose and what will appear in their background from classical Western art, but he presents the kinds of bodies rarely seen in them.

As I look at his Judith again, I wonder, is this how he found her? A woman going about her daily life when Wiley approached her with his unusual request? What about his Holofernes? Who is she? A specific kind of voter? The kind of woman we will see over and over in pandemic videos calling cops on her neighbors? Or perhaps the head is not human. Maybe this is a mannequin, and by slicing off her plastic head, this Judith—perhaps the owner of a retail store in a fashionable nook of North Carolina, or a regular shopper like you and me—is announcing that she is done with conversations about the ideal body type in American and, increasingly, global fashion. That she is clearing house, and ready for change.

I am struck by the artistic similarities between Artemisia and Wiley, though they are separated from each other by nearly 400 years. Just as Wiley wants us to see hitherto-unseen bodies posed powerfully in the tradition of Western classical art, Artemisia taught her audience to see women in a way they had never been seen before.

What else is the purpose of art if not to bridge the gap and create something fresh? Open our eyes to something we haven't considered yet?

WHEN I LOOK AT Wiley's *Judith and Holofernes*, it's impossible for me, a Bengali Hindu, to not see Kali. Though an atheist since fifteen, I remain socially and culturally rooted to the faith I was born into. I am fascinated by our mythology and iconography, especially when it comes to our goddesses and all they represent. If you learn to read iconography—the language of colors and symbols perfected over thousands of years—it's easy to tell who is who. Durga, as befitting her warrior status, rides a lion. Saraswati, the goddess of art and learning, carries the veena, a stringed musical instrument. Manasa, the "Mother of Snakes," bears snakes on her arms.

Kali always appears with a weapon—a sword, a scimitar, or even a trident. Both her name—from the Sanskrit *kaal*, meaning "time"— and her dark skin represent timelessness and infinity. She appears naked, with unruly black hair, but because she exists beyond our realm, our concepts of good, bad, pure, impure, pride, and shame do not apply to her.

I couldn't get enough of the goddess stories when I was growing up. I didn't have the language or sophistication to explain why, but the reason now seems apparent. Women righting an unfair world, teaching lessons to villains? What was not to love? I consumed those stories through books, TV shows, and my paternal grandmother. In thinking about Judith and Holofernes, I revisited several of these stories, including that of Kali confronting the demon Raktabija. His name, made up of two words, *rakta* (blood) and *bija* (seed), literally means "for whom each drop of blood is a seed." And indeed, for every drop of blood he sheds, a clone appears. In this way he replicates himself, again and again, until he fills the battlefield with himself, thus overwhelming his opponents.

Until Kali appears. In her most ferocious avatar, she enlarges her tongue and spreads it wide to catch every drop of Raktabija's blood so none can fall on the ground. Then she expands her mouth and swallows all of Raktabija's clones. Thus powerless, the once-powerful demon meets his end.

Perhaps it's the pandemic that makes me think this. What if Raktabija's blood represents our desires, in the way they multiply with no end? What if the battlefield where Raktabija and Kali confront each other represents our restless minds? Kali might be our reminder to live simply, to let go of the endless cycle of desire. She wants us to ask ourselves, maybe even in the language of Marie Kondo, whether this desire will "spark joy."

Perhaps Wiley's Judith is delivering a similar message. *Look me in the eye,* she commands. *Watch my sword as it arcs through air and lands right where it's supposed to. Do not be afraid. Look, there are flowers behind me, an entire Garden of Eden if you will, and I, a modern Eve, starting things anew.*

A CITY IN SEVEN METAPHORS

1. WILMINGTON IS "YOUR MAMA RAISED YOU RIGHT"

My teaching career in North Carolina begins with a weeklong orientation. For five days in a row, seventy or so of us new recruits gather inside a devastatingly gorgeous building that lulls us into thinking that every edifice on this campus must be made up of high ceilings, glass walls, and light fixtures one might see aboard a spaceship. That each classroom will not only be well appointed for teaching in the twenty-first century but will also display quaint markers of the past such as old-school wooden desks. A quotation from Francis Bacon—"Wonder Is the Seed of Knowledge"—shines over a set of pillars. I read it every time I walk to and from the presentations, which range from thirty minutes to two hours, on subjects as diverse as how to propose and teach a course abroad, how to sign up for health insurance, and what to do if an active shooter breaks into the classroom.

In between presentations, all of us new faculty members are fed lunch; offered tea, coffee, and snacks; and gifted coffee mugs, tote bags, and pens. An official photographer clicks individual and group photos for the newsletter and for our new university-issued identity cards.

The highlight of the week for me, however, is neither the keys to my new office nor shaking hands with the chancellor, but the three new colleagues I meet, all of whom teach in departments separate from mine, with expertise in subjects I know nothing about, yet offer me this particular praise on three unrelated occasions: "Your mama raised you right."

The first time it happens, I agree enthusiastically. Maybe it's the muggy August heat of Wilmington that's to blame, but I am convinced my new colleague wants to know more about my mother. I am about to launch into a lengthy lecture covering Ma's virtues when I notice her blue eyes take on a helpless, glazed look. She looks uncomfortable and wary. What-have-I-done-to-myself wary. Is-there-any-way-out-of-this-situation wary.

I stop. I have misread the signals. I must fix this and swiftly, lest I end up with a notoriety on this campus, perhaps even the entire state, where my mama, and by extension I, were subjects of jubilation just moments ago.

So I smile, and thank her—the compliment giver—and change the subject. *Won't she tell me, please, the name of her favorite restaurant in Wilmington.*

2. WILMINGTON IS SMILES, NODS, AND THE SAME CONVERSATIONS OVER AND OVER AGAIN

i. Yes, it IS so awesome that you went to India that one time and ate curry! No, that's all right, I don't need the recipe. We have only just met. It would be the same as me forcing my recipe for scrambled eggs on you without you asking for it.

ii. It makes me want to BURST with happiness that just because I complimented your dress as we were both entering the library, you found me two hours later, when I was settled deep in work, to tell me that you looked at the label and it turns out it was made in India. No, I don't recognize the dress. I think a lot of dresses must get made in India, no? There are 1 billion of us to clothe and keep decent. No, I didn't compliment your dress because I recognized the flowers. I just thought the print was pretty and summery. Yes, I think we have a lot of flowers in India.

iii. It is INSANE that your daughter-in-law's best friend from college is married to an Indian man! I am overjoyed that your son and daughter-in-law got to go to the wedding. There was dancing? And everyone wore nice clothes and ate delicious food? Oh, my, what a novel concept! Have you shared this finding with others? I firmly believe #normalizedancingatweddings should start trending on Instagram right about now.

iv. Of course, I am JUMPING with joy that you have discovered an amazing Indian sweet shop in Charlotte! Have you been felicitated yet? Does Columbus appear in your dreams and bestow on you the honor of "Best and Most Enterprising Explorer of All Time"? While he is at it, does he also rue the fact that there was no GPS during his time? Otherwise, surely he would have found the India he set out for. Damn those pesky maps and compasses!

3. WILMINGTON IS KNOBBED WHELK

It's my first Thanksgiving in Wilmington, and I don't want to spend it by myself. Just a month ago, the city gave me the scare of my life through its welcome gift of Hurricane Florence. After checking the weather app on my phone to verify that there are no hurricanes in my immediate future, I book myself a three-day stay at the same Atlantic Ocean–facing hotel where I was put up ten months ago when I interviewed for the job. Given that my room costs significantly less than it would in the summer, I naively assume this means that whenever I am not holed up in my room writing, I will roam empty hallways and enjoy miles of sandy beaches without another soul in sight. Everyone else will be at home, with family gathered around their dining tables, their mouths full of turkey, cranberries, and everything else that the Food Network insists must be cooked if you don't want to be annihilated by your loved ones on the day of the holiday.

I realize my mistake as soon as I arrive at the hotel. Long lines of guests wait impatiently outside the elevators, by the entrance to the in-house restaurant, and down by the private access paths to the beach, though the weather turns chilly.

On Thanksgiving morning, when I step out to the beach after breakfast, something pointy and sticking out of the sand catches my eye. It's brown and gray, perhaps a toy truck, its size comparable to a toddler's head.

I grab it by what feels like its horns and pull. So sure am I that it's made of plastic that I want to pop back into the hotel and toss it into their recycling bin. But the object is wedged deep, and heavier than I expected, no doubt with all the sand clogging up its insides. When I finally pry it out, it takes me a few minutes to rinse it in the waves puddling around my feet.

I hold it up in the sun, an unlikely Mufasa presenting an unlikelier Simba to the world. It's a shell. A real shell? No, that can't be. Surely, this object has known human design and intervention. Because if it's real, how has no one else grabbed it and taken it home? Especially on a crowded, urban beach like this, and given the shell's size and intactness? It certainly smells real, like at least twenty-five different creatures have died inside it, slowly, as if they were enjoying the process of coming to their end and did not want to rush it.

I bring the shell-not-shell up to my room. I wash it again, this time with soap, and place it on a chair in the balcony so it can dry out fully. Later, when I bring it back into the room and put it on my desk, it measures the same length as my Moleskin notebook. I look up the specifications: 8.25 inches. Mostly, I can't believe its gorgeousness—the whorls, the knobs on its shoulder, the delicate striations of orange and peach along its body, the pointed tip that's called the "apex." Surely this is a peace offering? It's the Atlantic Ocean apologizing for the terrible welcome of Hurricane Florence.

The next day, I photograph the shell from all possible angles. I post the pictures on Instagram so friends who are better informed than me on such matters can weigh in. Between them and my own online sleuthing, I identify what I have found: an adult, female, knobbed whelk shell. Apparently, whelks often function as males when young, and then *evolve* into females. The word choice makes me smile. Mostly, knobbed whelks live in cooler waters and feed on clams and oysters. I weigh her once I am back home: 398 grams or 14 ounces.

I name her—forgive me—Whelkie. These days, she lives in a drawer inside my writing desk, safe from prying, envious eyes. Every time I can't believe that I get to live fifteen minutes away from the ocean, I open the drawer, and Whelkie and I make eyes at each other.

4. WILMINGTON IS KIMCHI

White, blond, and nineteen, my student Nick is the son of a Baptist preacher father and a homemaker mother. They have family in Charleston, South Carolina, that they visit every summer. They have vacationed once in New York. They have never been abroad. Nick used to have a sister, but she died in an accident when she was little. I know these intimate details because Nick has shared them in the writing class that he is taking from me this fall.

Somewhere in the thick, heaving crowds that make up a college campus, and all the events that occur between the student union building, the auditoriums, the lawns, and halls, Nick has met and fallen in love with Julie. Julie is Korean, studies biology, and has long black hair. Nick and Julie have been together since spring, and it's going great. For his next essay, Nick is writing about Julie, and how his parents reacted when he told them that he was bringing his girlfriend home for Thanksgiving.

At first, they were delighted. Until the bit about her being Korean came up.

And Nick's father sighed and said, "Well, at least she's not Black."

And Nick's mother asked, "What will she eat? Does she smell of kimchi?"

Inside my office, Nick and I go over his essay. We discuss ways to revise, how and where to tweak so he can turn his frustration into art, and which literary journals he should send it to for possible publication.

In turn, I tell him about Kathy, the manager of the last building in which my husband and I lived in Idaho. Besides ours, there were eight other flats in the building. Kathy managed them all, and she lived in the unit right below ours. She had beautiful blue eyes and light blond hair. She loved gardening, and she was pleasant every time we ran into her in the elevator, the garage, or the stairs.

One evening, Kathy and I happened to be at the mail room at the same time. I had gathered my letters and was about to leave when Kathy asked, "How is your little boy?"

Now, I have never had, nor do I intend to have, either a little boy or a little girl. My confusion must have shown on my face. I watched Kathy's blue eyes widen with some sort of understanding, or recognition, because she blurted a quick "Sorry" and bolted from the room.

Later, while recounting the story to my husband, we realized what must have happened. Kathy had mistaken me for Ha-Yun, our next-door neighbor, and the only other woman of color in our nine-apartment building. Ha-Yun and I are about the same age and height. We both teach at the same university, albeit different subjects. Like me, Ha-Yun is married. Unlike my husband and me, though, Ha-Yun and her husband do have a little boy. The other relevant detail: Ha-Yun is from Seoul, South Korea, and not New Delhi, India.

If you didn't consider our faces, hair, language, food, and about fifty other categories, Ha-Yun and I could have been twins! No wonder Kathy got confused.

5. WILMINGTON IS CAROLINA WREN

On mornings when the breeze is like a caress, the bird feeder on my balcony fills up with chickadees, Carolina wrens, finches, titmice, and cardinals. The black-capped chickadees are no bigger than my thumb, yet their loud, disapproving calls can terrify the strongest among us. The titmice are on the other end of the spectrum. They are so quiet and polite; I worry for them in today's cutthroat world.

The finches visit us in groups of three and four. Occasionally there comes a loner who arrives and departs with others, yes, but eats a little distance from them. I suspect she is the memoirist of them all. Quietly observing everything only to publish an explosive tell-all book in a few months.

For a while I feel confident that the cardinals are my favorite. Especially the boy cardinals, with their majestic crests and vivid red breasts. Red has been my favorite color since I was five years old, and no trendy shade has ever dislodged it. I also appreciate that the way to a girl cardinal's heart is through food and that during courtship season, boy cardinals will not only bring their chosen girls seeds and grubs; they will also feed them to their beloveds with their own beaks, so much so that it will look like they are kissing. I learn that the cardinals are called so, and their Latin name is *Cardinalis cardinalis*, because their red color reminded early European settlers of the cardinals within the Catholic Church, with their uniform of red cassocks and caps. It bears logic, therefore, that a flock of red cardinals is called a "college," "conclave," or "Vatican."

But sadly, the cardinals don't seem impressed by either me or my husband. They only visit us when the feeder is full. Otherwise we are not worthy of their time.

Unlike the teeny-tiny Carolina wrens. Eager and inquisitive, with their brown tails shot up toward the sky, they possess an insatiable, indefatigable curiosity about the world, so much so that every time we change the location of a flowerpot or add a new plant, they inspect it from every angle.

Reluctantly I agree with my husband when he says, "Admit it, you have a new favorite. The wrens are the real deal. The cardinals are just flash and noise. Very little substance."

We also have a mockingbird, who visits occasionally and only eats blueberries; an especially persistent woodpecker that's convinced our balcony railing may yet be edible; and a shy blue jay whose status as Canada's national bird gets my Toronto-born husband very excited.

Wilmington is also mobs of geese. They live here year-round. They block traffic. They congregate in large numbers and amble through campus like it's theirs. They take their time crossing roads and streets. In certain parking lots at certain times of the day, they outnumber humans and cars combined.

6. WILMINGTON IS "WHAT DO THEY CALL YOU PEOPLE THESE DAYS?"

Our accountant—let's call him Monroe—is a chatty man in his fifties with little to no hair.

His scalp and forehead are forever shiny, like there are little light bulbs underneath his skin and any time he mentions words like "taxes" and "returns," they know to turn on and gleam bright. Though I have never touched him, besides once to shake his hand, I am confident that Monroe's skin is smooth like a porpoise. This is neither a fetish nor a judgment. It is simply a fact.

The first time we meet Monroe to discuss taxes and returns, he looks to my brown and bearded husband and asks, "And what is it that one calls people like you these days?"

My husband shrugs. Knowing his face and its expressions as well as I do, I can sense the tug of war between three different forces inside him: one that wants to forgive; a second that wants to educate; a third that wants to punch. The second force wins, and he tells Monroe, "Well, I was born in Canada and raised in California. My wife is from India. How about you call us North Carolinians for now?"

7. WILMINGTON IS FOURTH OF JULY ALONG THE CAPE FEAR RIVER

The Fourth of July is a big deal in Wilmington. There are concerts, symphonies, butterfly releases, 5K races, open houses, and, of course, robust fireworks over the Cape Fear River. An avalanche of tourists—we are talking tens of thousands—arrives every year to participate. Because I want to commit fully to where I live, I convince my husband to a staycation: we will rent a room in downtown Wilmington for two nights, just like out-of-town tourists, and enjoy everything the holiday has to offer. The first year we try this, we are too late. Reservations must ideally be made six months in advance. The only rooms still available come at an astronomical price. The next year, we try again, and this time we are successful. We acquire a room on the top floor of a downtown hotel, with a clear, uninterrupted view of the Cape Fear River.

We check into our room on July 3. It comes with a king-size bed. A desk. A framed photo on the wall that captures the Cape Fear River, the boardwalk, streetlights, and a boat in the distance. There is no other décor in the room, no suggestion that this is also a beach town. It's a peculiar relief, having stayed at Airbnbs along the North Carolina coastline that have adopted the nautical décor theme with aggression. Think welded metal fish sculpture in the bathroom; canvas prints of driftwood, beach umbrellas, and sand in the bedroom; a ship's wheel, usually distressed, on the outer wall; cotton rugs in stripes of navy and white; towels with sand dollar and starfish prints all over the house.

On this sunny summer afternoon, the Cape Fear River is the color of gold. Snowy egrets wade through the surrounding marsh, herons deep dive in search of food, and laughing gulls look like something unmentionable has gone down between two warring factions. What else explains why three of them are perched on one end of the observation deck with the fourth on the other, both sides keeping a safe and watchful distance from each other?

Beyond the water stands an abandoned house, straight out of a gothic novel. Who lived here? I want to know. When and why did they move away?

With the passing of every hour, the water keeps changing color: steel gray to metallic blue, muddy brown to monsoon green. Black ribbons streaked with silver. Or khaki pants left to soak for too long. No matter which direction my husband faces, and when, fish seemingly leap out of the water just for him. Every time he shouts, "Look, another one," I turn with what I think is lightning speed, but the leaping fish has done what it had to and disappeared.

"Why are you the chosen one?" I mutter. Between the two of us, I am the Bengali. I am the one who comes from a fish-(and rice)-for-every-meal eating culture. Unsurprisingly, Bengali folk art too is rife with fish motifs. When I was a kid, my grandfather would send me postcards every week that he illustrated with fish doing ludicrous things like smoking pipes, or wearing hats *and* smoking pipes, or going fishing. Since the pandemic, I have built up a daily art habit, and guess what I doodle, draw, and paint all the time? Fish. I make them with watercolors, acrylic markers, and gouache paints, but most often with whatever pen and pencil I have lying around. I paint them on canvas, I put them on bookmarks, I gift them to friends. And yet, despite my daily love and devotion, these ingrates won't put up a show for me?

WILMINGTON IS also the carefully restored battleship USS *North Carolina*, visible from our window and standing guard over downtown and the Cape Fear River. As its website will tell you, it is "the most highly decorated American battleship" of World War II. It "participated in every major naval offensive in the Pacific theater of operations, earning 15 battle stars." It's unexpected indeed, the sight of an actual, enormous battleship in a downtown crowded with couples holding hands, families with dogs, and restaurants, breweries, art galleries, and stores selling souvenirs. My husband has been to the battleship twice, both times with out-of-town friends and family. He wants to take me too. But I am not so keen yet.

On the first night of our staycation, we visit Cloud 9, the rooftop bar in the hotel next door. It offers a view of the glittering necklace of the city, and of fireworks prematurely being set off in the distance, concentric circles of red, gold, purple, and silver. What is it about this height that makes us feel hip, urban even, all things my husband insists we still are though we don't live in any of the gigantic cities in which we were born and raised? But can you truly be those things when the venue itself closes at the most unfashionable hour of 11 p.m.?

THE NEXT MORNING, it's the Fourth of July, and the breakfast buffet has all the expected accoutrements. The scrambled eggs are fluffy, the bacon crisp, and the breakfast potatoes taste better once you add hot sauce and ketchup. You may avail yourself of the make-your-own waffle station, and the toaster, should you want bread, bagel, or muffin. There's hot water if you want a cup of tea or a bowl of instant oats or grits. Add the brown sugar. Raisins. Walnuts and pecans. Preserved strawberries and jams. Butters, regular and peanut. The fridge contains four kinds of yogurt and two types of milk. A nifty dispenser in the corner spits out plastic knives, forks, and spoons. Inside the dining area, you may sit at one of the three round tables with four chairs apiece, or outside, where there is additional seating.

We sit inside. The lady at the table next to us is dressed in pink pants, white sneakers, and a white shirt with a busy print of red and blue shells, starfish, and mollusks. Her friend matches her energy with her own pink tank top and white shorts and starts what seems like will be a long story about her daughter and her life as a golf coach at a local high school. "Pam wasn't ever going to make it as a professional, Sue. She just wasn't. But look at her now. Finally, happy."

My husband and I aren't the only people staycationing. A man in denim shorts and blue shirt chats with the woman working the breakfast counter about the rising cost of living in Wilmington, and how he has been considering moving someplace else. Her black uniform contrasts in the most striking way with her ponytailed white hair, neatly tucked under a hair net. She nods and murmurs her agreement.

After breakfast we step outside the hotel, skirting around families about to go on river cruises, holding their huskies and poodles by the leash, posing for selfies that must somehow encompass it all—the sky, water, the bridge over the water, the boardwalk. A steady stream of boats makes its way down the river. Each flies the Star-Spangled Banner, whether as a nod to the occasion or because they do so every day, who can tell? The boat-owning demographic is the same over and over—white, middle-aged, or older, dressed in shorts, T-shirts, and hats.

Looking at this festive crowd and the surrounding celebrations, no one would think the Cape Fear River has been the site of so much violence. That an unknown number of Black bodies was dumped in these waters during the white-supremacist insurrection of 1898. Or when more than twenty-five inches of rain fell during Hurricane Florence in 2018 and water spilled over the banks, damaging nearby buildings and leaving a stench that lingered for months. Or that the Cape Fear River is the most industrialized river in all of North Carolina, lined with everything ranging from power plants to landfills. That it is polluted by, among other substances, Gen X, a chemical compound. Its presence in these waters served as the basis of the 2019 memoir *Exposure: Poisoned Water, Corporate Greed, and One Lawyer's Twenty-Year Battle against DuPont* by Robert Bilott, an environmental lawyer. The book in turn inspired the movie *Dark Waters*, a medical-legal thriller starring Mark Ruffalo.

My husband and I heard about Gen X from our apartment manager on our first day in Wilmington. He cautioned us against drinking the tap water, which is why even now, four years later, we have filtered water delivered to our home that we use for drinking and cooking.

When the sky darkens in the afternoon, we retreat to the hotel. For the next couple of hours, it rains like there is no end in sight. Like the fireworks will have to be canceled. But just as unexpectedly, the rain stops, and the weather turns beautiful.

"The gods want us here," I tell my husband. "They are glad we are doing this."

He agrees. "To be able to walk around Wilmington in July without sweating is a miracle indeed."

We go out to the riverwalk and find ourselves a bench. Nothing can come between us and the fireworks, though they are still a couple of hours away. Until then, there is people-watching. Parents with strollers. Parents who have dressed themselves and their children in matching outfits, right from the patriotic-themed hats down to the shoelaces. Several folks have brought their dogs with them. Aren't dogs supposed to be afraid of fireworks, though?

I whisper to my husband, "I'm scared."

"Why? You love fireworks."

"What if a gunman shows up?"

"We'll be fine." He holds my hand.

A baby in a passing stroller glares at my husband. We giggle. I tell him, "The baby knows you're up to no good."

The fireworks show is even better than I expected. Bolts of gold, silver, red, purple, green, and fuchsia streak the sky, their reflections sparkling off the Cape Fear River. When it ends, a group of men sitting directly behind us screams into the smoke-filled night, "'Merica! Brexit! Greatest nation! I love the smoke from fireworks!"

I study them warily. Are they armed? Are they about to do something? I nudge my husband toward our hotel. As our distance grows from them, I pray that with their oversized hats, baggy clothes, and foam fingers, the men look threatening but really are just ridiculous.

On the elevator ride back to our room, we meet a husband and wife in their sixties who are visiting Wilmington from Athens, Georgia.

"Did you enjoy the fireworks?" I ask.

"Enjoy?" The husband says. "Darling, we have been coming here for the last nineteen years."

"Nineteen?"

"Yes! Wilmington is our favorite city."

"Wow! We like Athens too. We have a friend who lives there." The elevator pulls to a stop on our floor.

"Perhaps we know your friend! What's his name?"

The elevator door closes as I'm trying to figure out whether to divulge our friend's name to absolute strangers.

"Nineteen years," my husband whispers as he unlocks the door to our room. "Why? Aren't there fireworks in Athens or anywhere else in Georgia?"

The next morning, at breakfast, I see the wife of the Athens couple. Dressed in an orange kaftan and beige Crocs, she sets two plates on a tray and goes about filling them up, clearly intending to take it back to their room.

When I say hi and remind her of our chat the night before, she tells me more of their story. Somewhere during their years of coming to Wilmington, their son fell in love with a local girl. Now they are married, with children. The grandchildren and the fireworks make for two excellent reasons to visit Wilmington every July. They always stay in this very same hotel, in their preferred room, 408. Its position is such that they can watch the fireworks from the window if they want, in the comfort of the air conditioner. Last night's show was twenty-five minutes long. Last year's was twenty-two and a half minutes. Across from the water, there is another fireworks show in Leland. All the old employees at this hotel know them. They are like family. And of course, the breakfast is fabulous.

When we return to our room to gather our items and finish packing, my husband hits the shower. I draw close to the window, to take in the slow traffic of boats, egrets, and seagulls one last time. Far out in the river, a flock of handout-seeking long-billed pelicans surrounds a red and white fishing boat. Just then, as if on cue, as if only for me, a fish leaps out of the water.

ACKNOWLEDGMENTS

THANKS TO THE EDITORS OF *Chautauqua, Hunger Mountain, Blood Orange Review, Crab Creek Review, Michigan Quarterly Review, Arkansas International, IDAHO* magazine, and the anthologies *We Are the River, A Harp in the Stars,* and *South to South: Writing South Asia in the American South* for publishing previous versions of some of these essays.

Thanks to my wonderful agent, Sally Wofford-Girand, for guiding me through the process. A million thanks to my editor, Cate Hodorowicz, who has been an incredible powerhouse of support and encouragement, and to the entire team at UNC Press—Mary Caviness, Sonya Bonczek, Liz Orange, Lindsay Starr, and others—for taking such excellent care of my book every step of the way.

A million thanks to my editor, Cate Hodorowicz, who has been an incredible powerhouse of support and encouragement. Many thanks to the entire team at UNC Press for taking such excellent care of my book every step of the way.

I am also deeply appreciative of my colleagues and students at the University of North Carolina Wilmington. Most days, I can't quite believe that I get to talk books, writing, and storytelling for a living.

Much of this book was written at Randall Library, UNCW, and I thank the universe for this inspiring space and its excellent staff.

A shout-out to dear friends Annie Lampman, Jamaica Ritcher, Tara Roberts, Katie Farris, and Jeff Jones. Thank you for being in my life.

A creative person can neither exist nor flourish in a vacuum. I am thankful to the community that keeps me buoyed up: Amrita Das, Lauris Burns, Aris Harding, Heather Wilson, Sara Allen, and Sally Reavis.

Like my previous books, this one wouldn't exist without the love and support of my parents, Swapna and Atanu Dasgupta. Many thanks, Ma and Baba. Cheers also to my brother Aritro and sister-in-law Ashmita. To my grandparents, I miss you all very much. Thank you for your stories and indulgences.

Finally, all my love and gratitude to my husband, Amrinder Grewal. Thank you for being on this brown woman's team!

Printed in the USA
CPSIA information can be obtained
at www.ICGtesting.com
LVHW042120270824
789273LV00005B/141